RAKINGS UP

FAR HEY, FRIARMERE

RAKINGS UP

An Autobiography

AMMON WRIGLEY

E. WRIGLEY & SONS LTD., ROCHDALE
Publishers

FIRST PRINTING 1949

PRINTED IN ENGLAND BY
E. WRIGLEY & SONS LTD.
ROCHDALE.

PREFACE

An autobiography is generally awaited with keen interest and "Rakings Up" will I trust convey to the reader the pattern of Ammon Wrigley's life, particularly in his early years.

In discharging the request that I should write this preface, I feel that the story is far from complete when looking back over the last thirty years. Events and anecdotes regarding Ammon Wrigley and his friends come into my mind that have not found a place in this book. "Rakings Up" suggests an effort to gather and record the memories of a lifetime, and when Ammon Wrigley commenced to write his narrative he was over 80 years of age— faculties had begun to fail, and the once vibrating memories had become fainter, leaving the power of reminiscence impaired. The gradual decline in health with all its attendant ills made the writing of this autobiography difficult for the writer, and with a sense of relief he completed it, and gave explicit instructions regarding its publication.

Ammon Wrigley had a long life, spending a good deal of his time tramping the moors, and in research relating to Saddleworth. The result of his diligence was enhanced with the gift to write and publish the numerous books which are so much sought after to-day. His writings will remain a link between the calmer bygone days of handloom weavers, farmers and mooredgers, and the bustling industrial rush of to-day.

Ammon Wrigley was born on the mooredge—he roamed the hills, and his last request was that his ashes be returned to the moors. On September 14th, 1946, his ashes were scattered according to his instructions near the Dinner Stone on Millstone Edge, at the head of the Castleshaw Valley in Saddleworth by Mr. Harry Walne, the President of The Ammon Wrigley Fellowship, who along with Mr. Harold Whitworth, Hon. Secy., was instrumental in promoting the erection of a commemorative Bronze Tablet adjoining the last resting place. A little couplet from his poem "An Old Shepherd" reminds me of what he wished.

"Clean and sweet about thee lies,
The rolling moors, the open skies."

S. SEVILLE.

Waterhead, Oldham.

CONTENTS

ILLUSTRATIONS

INTRODUCTION

I have been described in books and national newspapers as an "unschooled millworker", a description that surely fits, for as boy and a man I did manual work in various mills for sixty years. At last I fell through a trap door in a mill warehouse and as I did not bounce it ended my working days. It has been stated that I have published a greater variety of books and booklets about my native parish than any other lifelong millworker in Lancashire has published about his parish. How far this is true or otherwise I neither know nor care. I often think that I have been too much interested in local historical and antiquarian work, and might have done better if I had written nothing but verse and folk tales. Much of my best verse was written at Beswicks with a pencil on poor paper and when we moved to Hilltop many were so badly faded with having been rummaged about in a drawer that I could not read them and they were burnt.

I have more sense than to claim that I have written poetry. I am merely a minor versifier among the thousands of men and women who are now contributing to magazines and newspapers much better verse than mine. I have never read what I call poetry without thinking I ought to burn my own, but it might put the fire out. If there is any value in my verse it is in "Men of the Churchside" and other poems that describe the bygone social and industrial life of Saddleworth. I have seen cottage spinning, warping, sizing, weaving and other processes that the parish may never see again. In "Those Were the Days" there is a long list of Saddleworth cottage manufacturers in 1797.

The folk tales in my books were gathered from old inn corners and from the hearths of farmers and handloom weavers on the mooredges. Some of the tales they had heard from their fathers and mothers, and when I said they seemed stretched I was always assured that they were true. I have never voted at a Parliamentary or District Council election as I knew little about them and cared less. On two occasions I had the chance of becoming a somebody, but I refused to allow my name to be sent up to London. I told the gentleman who had proposed it that my name was good enough for me without a J.P. appendage. I have not seen a play or an opera, and only been twice to the pictures.

I know nothing about what is called "writer's craft", and I am just as dense about "style". I have taken no pains and the reader will soon find a handful of slips. My pen has always galloped along in a hurry to reach the end. Yet Mr. J. H. Swann in his lecture on my work given before the Manchester Literary Club said "He writes in a clear natural style which carries the reader along untiringly. He describes what he sees realistically and is yet alive to the beauty and poetry of nature. There is nothing forced in his descriptions. He is not merely the literary delineator, he has experienced what he sets down". If I am all that, it is more than I knew and—

"What I have writ is writ,
Whether it be blest or curst,
Remember the little that's good
And forgive and forget the worst".

I believe there is a streak of Rabelais in me, just enough to keep me goody goody mortal. In one of his books Samuel Butler says "God does not like people to be too good, and that it is more pardonable with Him to be a little too bad".

I have gone through life more carelessly than I might have done, and though at times the road was rough, I managed to keep the right foot first and jogged along.

Men seek happiness in countless ways, but I have ever loved the quiet ways of life. I have had no worries about creeds or politics, and cared nothing for isms, cults or ologies, but I have cared everything for homely dalesfolk and for hills, moors and all little things that live in the open air. They have kept April green in my heart and taken me out roaming and singing my songs into the winds.

> I love a friend, a song and a glass,
> Gaily along life's road I pass.
> Joyous and free out of doors for me
> Over the hills in the morning.

Ammon Wrigley.

This book is Dedicated with affection and remembrance
to my five grandchildren.

Mary Pulfer (nee Wrigley).
Alice Sidebottom (nee Wrigley).
John Ammon Seville.
Mary Wrigley Smith.
Ruth Elizabeth Seville.

RAKINGS UP

ANCESTRY

The little I know about my paternal forbears, is, that they were small farmers and handloom weavers on the Friarmere hills, a bare bleak district in West Yorkshire. A Willelmus Wryglegh appears in a roll dated 1379. and in 1524 a John Wrigley held a farm on Friarmere and paid a rent of two pounds a year to the Monastery of Roche near Rotherham. He may have been an ancestor of mine, but it is more than I can prove.

My great grandfather was James Wrigley of Hey, a farmstead in the Denshaw district, that now stands among its withered fields like a miserable old scarecrow of a building unfit for human habitation. He was a shy quiet man who pottered about his shippon with a muckfork and talked more to cows than he did to humans. For all his shyness, he married Rachel Rhodes, one of the Warrock Hill breed, a big rawboned woman who could do almost every kind of farm work, even to mowing with a scythe.

She ruled the house in a masterful way, and the three sons did as they were told with once telling. When they were old enough to spin and weave she began making cloth, and as the business head of the house did all the buying and selling. When two pieces had been woven she took them to Huddersfield to be sold in the grease. In frock and petticoats she rode there, "stroddle leg" (astride) on a white horse with the pieces strapped on its back behind her. In those days it would be an unusual sight to see a woman astride a horse, and she might get plenty of ridicule as she passed through the villages, but they would not have their own way, for she had a rough and ready tongue, and laid about them in a wordy duel. Many Saddleworth cottage manufacturers took their greasy cloths to Huddersfield market, but none would be better known than Rachel o' th' Hey. My father used to say that his gronnie had told hundreds of people that her "hund" was raw with riding without a saddle, and I heard my Uncle Jim say that when he went to see his gronnie in winter, he always looked through the window before going to the door, and often saw her standing at the fire warming her bare buttocks.

Their son James Wrigley, better known in the dales as Jamie o' Rachel's, was my grandfather. A lover of sport, he kept a gamecock for fighting and a hound for hunting, and went to Heights Church on Sunday mornings in tall silk hat and sober black cloth, and no vicar's warden ever went in at its door with more impressive dignity. In his heyday he was huntsman to the Friarmere pack, and rarely missed a hunt after he had resigned. If the hounds came by his farm when he was sat at dinner, he jumped up from his chair, threw the food out of his mouth into the fire, and rushed out to join in the chase. On election days, he tied a weaver's blue apron to a long sizing stick, and stuck it out of a bedroom window. Then he went out into the lane and shouted "hip, hip, hooray" for the Tories till he could be heard at all the farms and cottages on the hillside.

RALPH BROADBENT

He had married Martha Broadbent, the sister of Ralph Broadbent, who kept a boarding school at his farm on the hill above Heights Church. It still stands 1,100 feet above the sea level, and in his day it became famous over a wide area of industrial Lancashire, not only for teaching, but also for the way he fed his boarders. They lived on the best fare that his farm could produce. Milk warm from the cow, new butter from his own churn, new laid eggs, home made cheese, home fed ham and bacon, and home grown vegetables. At holiday times they went home shining

16

MARY WRIGLEY

THOMAS WRIGLEY

with good health, which served to give the school a good name. Of course the clean fresh air from the moors kept his scholars hungry and hearty, and a few who had begun their schooling under Ralph Broadbent became Members of Parliament. He was not only a schoolmaster, farmers knew him as the best cow doctor in the parish, and he made pills for human ailments. I am said to have got my love of books from the Broadbents.

WRIGLEYS

The Wrigley's had plenty of hard work in their lives. Their destiny was to come into the world with a spade in one hand and a weaver's shuttle in the other. They were called "wheelbarrow farmers" or men who could not afford a horse, but managed to keep a cow or two and weave a bit of cloth. Bred and born on the wild mooredge, they cared little for wind and rough weather, and the women thought nothing of getting out of bed on a winter's morning and setting their feet in a snowdrift on the chamber floor. They appear to have believed in the old adage "What I spent I had, and what I saved I lost", and made straight with what they got, and left the next generation to work for itself, which kept the breed from getting dry rot and becoming worm eaten. They were musical; one was an organist; another played the flute in Heights Church, and my Aunt Lucy was a famous singer and often engaged as the principal soloist at church festivals. One Sunday, along with a friend "Moll o' mi Gronnie's" she went to sing at Hey Chapel near Lees, and when they were having tea with Parson Grundy he kept pressing Moll to take a little celery, and at last she said, "Aw'll just try a rhism, but it's first time Mr. Grundy 'at aw've had white rhuberb".

My forbears gave me no worldly goods, not even a yard of land or a thimble full of gold. They hadn't them to give, but they gave me something that I would not sell for money, even if I could. Their gifts were all in the rough and I have not tried to polish them, and perhaps if I did try, I might make them look

17

like sham things. They gave me a love for all that is honest, clean and above board, and a deeply rooted hatred for all kinds of sham, pretence and make believe. They loved the quiet ways of life, but not more than I do. My father was the only one to carry a gun for wild fowling, a sport that I disliked, for I have ever loved wild birds, wild flowers, and all little things that live in fields, pools and running waters. I think a working man with a love for the countryside and its wild life is in a way well off, for it is something that sweetens his life. So loving beautiful things I have gone through life much happier than if I had lived for nothing but scraping money together.

MY FATHER

My father Thomas Wrigley was the youngest of ten children, all brought up upon thick home made oatcake, milk from their father's cows, and oatmeal porridge with plenty of spring water and fresh air, so no wonder they were healthy. In the summer months the younger end ran wild in the hilly fields on the mooredge. They were brown as gipsies, bareheaded and sometimes barefooted, and at bedtime their father got his cow crutch and having rounded them up like sheep, they ran homewards racing and shouting along the hillside. They slept in the loom chamber with pack sheets and old meal sacks hung across it to divide the lads from the lasses. In houses where there were children of both sexes the parents slept in the living room on a press bed. That kind of bed was panelled on the under side, and when it was closed up in the daytime it looked like a wardrobe.

My father grew up tall and straight as an ash sapling, with good use of his limbs. Though we were poor he had a light heart, and on winter nights he would sit in his old rush bottomed chair and sing for an hour at a stretch. He had a light foot, and was so fine a dancer that with a woman partner he always led off the old country dances that were then held in the club rooms of the village inns. He won at ribbon dances, in which eggs were laid on the floor and the dancers had to avoid breaking them. The prize was a length of silk ribbon and the winner was very proud of it, as only good dancers ventured to take parts in the competitions, and some women wore the ribbon round their bonnets. As a young man he ran eleven match sprint races, winning ten and losing his last to Emmanuel Fitton of Shaw. Most of his races were run before large crowds on the level stretch of the Huddersfield main road at New Delph.

He was a member of an Oddfellows Society in the village and at its meetings he often sung a humourous song called "The Oddfellow's Wife". It described how the wife of an Oddfellow was continually nagging her husband to tell her how he was made an Oddfellow. What rites and ceremonies were performed before he became a member. At last he decided to try and stop her tongue and make her an Oddfellow. She had to get a number of articles and I can only remember one verse

> "Awst want a lot o' curious things,
> Locks an' bowts an' keys an' springs,
> A pair o' new kilt pigeon wings,
> And a little kitchen poker ;
> Of books she borrowed a gradely lot,
> Byron, Burns, an' Walter Scott,
> Shakespeare, Milton, Pope an' Knott,
> This making is no joker...."

When she had got everything he required, he laid her face downwards on the carpet, and piled the things over her. Then he touched her bare buttocks with the warm poker till she screamed, and it brought peace to the house.

HOUND CHRISTENING

My father was always fond of sport, and one Sunday afternoon I went with him to a christening of hound whelps. Times have changed since many Saddleworth farmers and a few handloom weavers kept a hound, and it was an easy matter to get a pack together. In those days men believed that "every lad worth rearing was hunting bred and born" and I have heard it told that after a hunting day John Andrew washed his two hounds like little children and put them into one of his beds. He was a hunstman and kept the inn at Saddleworth Church. Sometimes just before a match trail was run, the hound and the trail runner slept in the same bed so that they could get the smell of each other and become inseparable companions.

The christening took place at the house of an old hunter, who had loved hounds from his cradle and may have been like Jamie o' Topper's

"When he wur as fine a child
As ever blest a mother,
He lay i' th' cradle at one end
An' a grand heaund whelp at tother".

I was present through the influence of my father, for only old seasoned hunters were permitted to witness the christening of hounds. A great bowl of punch and a number of wine glasses stood in the middle of the table. The high priest was the huntsman, Allen Schofield, better known as Allen o' th' Tinker's, who sat in his red coat at the head of the table. On his right sat the whipperin, Joe o' Breb's, who went out of the room and returned with a whelp and placed it into Allen's hand as gently as ever a mother placed a sleeping child in a cradle. When Allen had looked in the whelp's face he said :—

"Theau mun be a good dog an' true to thi mester. Theau munnot worry ducks nor chickens nor nowt wi' fithers on. Theau munnot run cats, nor sheep, nor ceaws, but theau mun run a hare as lung as thi legs 'ill carry thi. Theau mun keep thi nose cowd an' thi tail op an' theau munnot go marlockin wi curs an' other low bred dogs. Awm beawn to co thi Plunder an' hope theau'll be a credit to thi fayther an' mother an' o belungin to thi".

He poured a little punch on its head, and pulled its ears till it yelped and proved there was music in its mouth. He then dipped the toes of its forefeet in the punch. They had been washed, and the hunters filled their wine glasses and drank to Plunder. It was said that dipping hardened their feet for running over frozen ground.

COCKFIGHTING

We kept gamecocks and allowed them to fight for Yorkshire in the great mains against Lancashire. It was then, as now, an illegal sport, but I only remember one fight that was broken up by the police. It took place on Stanedge moors, and two of my father's friends, both fat innkeepers, began to run away and always said, "If we hadn't started a woakin we should ha' been catched". My father never saw his cocks fight for he had to stay at his work in the mill, but cockfighters used to sit round our hearth and describe the fights, and talk about brown reds, black reds, hard feather, snake like heads and other points about cocks, till I longed to see a fight and at last I did. My father died in his 56th year, and I allowed our last cock to fight and it won in two mains for Yorkshire, but got blinked in a fight that took place in a wood near Huddersfield. An old cockfighter brought it home in a sack and when he rolled it out on to the floor I could see neight head nor tail. It was the shape of a Rugby football, and the cockfighter said, "It wur a very hard feight agen a cock fro Manchester, an' it's swelled wi being cut wi' th' spurs, but it kilt t'other cock". In one of my books I describe a cockfight on the moors that was almost as quiet and orderly as a prayer meeting.

At one time it was the sport of kings, and Charles II gave Nell Gwynn a pair of silver cockspurs with her initials stamped on them. In 1654, Lord Roos and ladies went from Haddon Hall to a cockfight at Bakewell, and Sir George Vernon took two pounds from the Household purse at Haddon and went to a cockfight at Ashbourne. In a book entitled "The Cocker" written by W. Sketchley, gent., and published in 1814 he says,

"In the years 1786 and 1788 I bought 30 fighting cocks from the Rev. Mr. Brooks of Shiffnal, Shropshire". He would be red nosed, and probably took his choir and congregation with him when he went to a cockfight.

MY MOTHER

I know next to nothing about my mother's ancestry. Her maiden name was Mary Waddington, and it is said that the family sprung from Waddington; a charming village between Clitheroe and the Trough of Bowland. Her branch spread out Halifax way and married with Bancrofts and Holdsworths who were quarry folks on the Ovenden hills. All that I know about those relations is, that one quarryman drank a pint of rum for a wager and died from alcoholic poisoning. They are buried in the bleak weathered churchyard of St. Mary's at Illingworth. When my grandfather Waddington moved from Morley to Huddersfield, my mother came to Delph in Saddleworth, to be a servant to an elderly maiden lady. She was then 15 years of age, and had never known a day's schooling, but at Delph she found a kind mistress who taught her to read and write. At that time the village was a poor place, and when she threw apple skins on to the midden behind the house the children fought for them. The inns were open all night, and men who were too drunk to go home, slept with their heads and arms on the taproom tables, and in the morning she often saw angry wives tearing through the village to shake their fists at the taproom windows.

My mother grew up to be a good woman, and I remember her with deep and lasting reverence. She was the shyest and gentlest creature that I have ever known. Words never came from a kinder tongue, or from one that was less used for gossiping. She hated to be told scandal and never retold it, and though not wanting in neighbourly friendliness, she kept as much as possible under her own roof. I remember her trying to drive sense into a neighbour woman who one morning had given birth to a child, and on the following morning got out of bed, went into the shippon and helped her husband to milk seven cows. All done that she could boast about it to other women. My mother was a healthy woman and turned sixty before she had a bottle of medicine. In the hard toiling years of her early married life, she said to one of my aunts, "I want no girls, I hope all my children are boys", and they were,—she had five,—three dying in infancy.

On her wedding day my mother came from Huddersfield to Diggle station, and my father met her there, and as they walked the two miles over a hill and through a valley to Heights Church the women came out of laneside cottages and gave them the customary greeting, "Good husband, good wife, pratty childer an' big puddings". My mother heard it with downcast eyes, and was glad when she got inside the Church. In the afternoon they went to Hollingworth Lake, at that time called the "weavers' seaport", and it was late when they reached home at Oxhey, a now ruined house that stands on the lane leading to Friarmere Moors. My mother had never been inside the sleeping rooms of handloom weaver folks and I often heard her tell what kind of a bedroom she found on her wedding night.

"I had pictured a homely little bedroom with lime washed walls, old fashioned furniture, carpeted floor and white curtains to the windows. When I reached the top of the stairs with a candle in my hand I was never more shocked in my life. As far as I could see from the doorway it was a dreary old barn more fit for cows than for humans. The candle gave a poor light and as I peered into the room I saw a bed near a handloom, and on one side there was a little chair. Trembling with fear I went to the chair on tiptoe. The pillow and bed covers were clean and a piece of coarse sacking served for a carpet. I had sat on the chair for a few minutes when I thought I heard something stir in one of the dark corners of the room, and I jumped to my feet and almost screamed with fright. I had just undressed when I chanced to look towards the windows and was startled

23

to see that they were without curtains. I rushed to the candle to put it out, but I had no matches to re-light it. I went to the windows and looked out. There was not a light to be seen neither on the hillsides nor in the valley. Nothing but darkness and no sound but the wind from the moors moaning about the lonely old house. When I thought of the little bedroom at Huddersfield, and how I heard people talking and laughing as they went home from the theatre, I began to cry and tears ran down my face as I said my prayers. I afterwards knew that children were born among looms, for bed and workroom were one in most cottages. I have seen the dead in their coffins between looms, and in the old watermills a corner of the cardroom was partitioned off for the carder and his family to live in. I knew one old couple who lived in a mill and slept in a bag of wool as they had no bed".

One of my uncles had lived in the house at Oxhey, and left a loom for my father, but he was working at Denshaw mill, as rotten a hole as ever fouled the green earth of Saddleworth. His wages were twelve shillings a week, and when he received them, my mother had to spend what she required in groceries at a shop kept by the mill master. Some weekends he received a piece of cloth instead of money, and then he had to tramp to Oldham and Rochdale and sell for what he could get. Other people worked at Denshaw mill under the same degrading and illegal conditions. I could give the name of the mill master, but it might make my page stink like a polecat. In old directories you will find the hellish combination "manufacturer and shopkeeper", and when such men died the world was well rid of them, and the air purer when they had ceased to breathe it. My mother knew that his wages of twelve shillings would keep her back bare and her teeth clean, so my father left Denshaw mill and they went to live at Far Hey, a storm battered old house that is now in ruins. He began to weave for another manufacturer and my mother learned to spin on a fifty spindled jenny.

24

MILLCROFT, CASTLESHAW VALLEY

A neighbour woman had a forty spindled jenny and it had become almost unworkable. The manufacturer replaced it with one of fifty spindles, but the woman said "forty spindles are as mony as aw con watch" and she had always ten spindles running empty. For a time my parents must have done fairly well for one of my aunts said that my father sang all day at his work.

WHOOPING COUGH

My mother told me that when I was two years old I had a severe attack of whooping cough. She said we got no sleep and were not fit for work in the morning. Every remedy from a chemist's shop in the village had been tried but they gave me no relief, and one fine day she wrapped me in a shawl and my father carried me in his arms over the moors to Badger Slacks. There was a strong wind blowing in my face, and when he had taken me back home, my cough was cured. So it is no wonder that I love the moors. They were blown into me on that day, and have never been blown out.

When about five years old, we left Far Hey, and went to live at Millcroft in the Castleshaw valley, in those days one of the loveliest hamlets in the parish. My father had become a spinner and my mother a piecer at a woollen mill a few fields away. The grass is now green where that mill once stood, and people pass and never dream that it was once the site of a shoddy poverty making hellhole.

THE CASTLESHAW VALLEY

The dalesfolk called early boyhood days "apple pie days" and so they are, but gone all too soon, and looking back on that valley as I first knew it, I see all that I have ever known of life's fairyland. Coming in spring from the bleak treeless fields and black stone walls of Far Hey, to Millcroft with its trees, gardens, fields and meadow hedges filled my young eyes with wonder and delight. I still see the sunshine in that pleasant valley, the hawthorn blossom, the first time that I had seen white trees, the pools and marshy places yellow with kingcups. In summer, blackberry on the hedges, raspberry, wild rose and honeysuckle in the cloughs, and wimberry on the moor. Nothing to do in the sunny weather but go birdnesting in April and May, and then wander home sunburnt, with holes in my stocking heels, a torn coat, and my mother saying "here he comes black as the dule's hoof and ragged as a filly foal". The valley has changed since my young days. Its upper reaches are now sealed up by large water-works belonging to a Lancashire town, and the mills, farms, cottages and the old families that occupied them are gone for ever. The once rich meadowlands are overgrown with rushes and rank grasses, and the once well trod fieldpaths can scarcely be traced from one stile to another. It is a sad end to the toil of bygone farmfolk who with spade and plough had wrested their lands from the moor.

If I wished to see a countryside that looks heartbroken I would go to the Castleshaw valley and wander among its lone forsaken fields and meadowlands, over broken flagstones that had once formed the floors of farm and cottage, over broken field walls and ragged hedges never to be repaired. Up grass grown lanes, by old hawthorns that had enclosed well kept gardens, I might set my feet on the grass where a hearthstone had been, and where I had sat with a farmer and his wife to "brewis" after a housing day. I might find a lark's nest on the very spot where I had heard a mother croon cradle songs to her children, and gather harebells where old Bonker used to sit on the wall with his clay pipe and a pot of home brewed ale ; a dim quiet figure in the summer dusk. I would go to a well that is choked with mud and rubble. A row of weavers' houses once stood near it, and who could guess how many puddings and dumplings had been boiled in its water or how many bowls of broth, cups of tea and gallons of home brewed ale it had made. Nor can anyone guess how many hearty lads and bonnie lasses had washed their faces with its water during the past one hundred years. I have written verses about that well, but I cannot lay my hands on them. I remember that I told how its waters tinkled like little bells and made the sweetest music on that hillside lane. How Mally took her blue pitcher to the well when she made rum and tea. How old Joe Raggle made his richest broth from its water, and he said there were more stars of fat on the top than there were stars in the skies. Betty o' Ab's always brewed her Wakes and Christmas ales with its water though she had to carry it across three fields. It was said that the farther the brewing water had to be carried and the shorter the measure to the peck the stronger the ale. Betty used to tell the young men to sup at that well when they went a courting if they wished to get good wives, and so on for about ten verses. For all its silence and desolation the Castleshaw valley is the dearest bit of earth I have ever known.

HOME REMEDIES

I remember when a little boy at Millcroft had measles my brother and I had to go and play with him so that we could catch the infection and have it at the same time. I believe the medicine was liquid yeast from home brewed ale. Up to being about ten years old I had to go to bed with a cow dung plaster round my neck as a cure for sore throat. My father used to fetch the dung out of the shippon just as it fell warm from the cow. It was plastered on a piece of flannel and then tied round my neck. Another common remedy was a collop of fat bacon tied round the neck, and I knew an old farmer who always had his neck collop fried for his breakfast, but I had to have cow dung because we had no bacon. There were two old handloom weavers lived near us, both widowers, and when they went out seeking second wives they always rubbed their faces with new butter to make them shine. Another old weaver was said to wash his face with "lant" urine, and no young girl had a fairer skin. When Dick o' th' Hey was mellow with ale he would come singing down the lane and get over a wall into a field. Then he would kick a cow up and go to sleep in the warm grass where it had been laid.

SCHOOLING

When about seven years old I began to go to the little mooredge school at Castleshaw, at that time one of the busiest and merriest farming and weaving hamlets in the parish, and in the evening noisy with children playing in the lane. Now, where there had been the warmth and stir of life for 400 years, there is silence and ruin. The teacher was a young woman who came from a Lancashire town, but she had a short stay. The school committee said that she did not like the wild moorland district, the rude dialect and the strange nicknames of the weaver folks.

When she had gone another young woman became our teacher, but she could not master the big moorland lads and every noonday a farmer's son made ugly drawings of her on a blackboard. When she left a hamlet woman was our teacher. She had kept a dame school and could only teach the infants, and the big boys and girls did as they pleased. The infants brought their school pence stitched in one corner of their "bishops" or pinafores, and on a Monday morning she was busy cutting the stitches loose. I loved going to that school for in summer we played truant and went on the moor gathering wimberries.

The school was closed many years ago and in one of my books I have described the poverty and the sad end of the last teacher. One cold windy day I went down the moor to the school, and the only living thing in sight was a kestral hawk hovering over a bleak pasture. The wind was wuthering mournfully against the school walls, a fitting wind for so dreary a place. I looked through the school windows blurred with green moss and cobwebs. The lime had dropped from the ceiling and lay in dirty patches on the floor, and among the thick dust on the desks were torn leaves of spelling books and broken inkpots.

A blackened rain soaked old map lay on the floor below some broken windows, and a few tattered prints of lions, tigers and other animals were hanging askew on the walls. The soot had fallen down the chimney into the rusty little firegrate and covered the hearthstone. I went down the school yard for I had seen things that would give me unpleasant memories, and going along the empty lane I thought of the time when the school was the hub of the dale, and all kinds of merry makings and folk gatherings were held under its roof, tea parties, dances, concerts, Easter, Whitsuntide and Christmas festivities.

People who lived in that happy time would never dream how soon and how sad a future would come to that valley and the school.

I disliked going to the Sunday school, for when I had been pent up all week inside four walls I longed to be out of doors at the weekends roaming alone over Friarmere moor, and I slipped away when I could, and never got a prize for good attendance. One winter I went to a night school at Delph, and learned nothing. I should have been better at home writing rhymes. I have a memory of going to that school that has nothing to do with teaching, but I had heard neighbours whisper eerily about boggarts till I was easily scared when out of doors at night. How they had red eyes as big as dinner plates, and chased people up the dark hillside lanes.

THE OLD MILL

With no moon, the rough winding path by the brook and along the narrow unfenced embankment of a dam was one of some danger, and a false step where the path turned near a weir pool would have hurled me plunging into deep black waters. Yet the only thing I feared apart from boggarts was the loud rumbling noise of the waterwheel at Hull mill, and my way led close through its yard. It was a black fearsome looking building that had been untenanted for years and the greasy old rooms were empty. The mullioned windows were green with moss and dirty with tattered cobwebs. The buckets had not been disconnected, and the big waterwheel turned at short intervals day and night. I did not like to hear it turn in the daytime, for coming suddenly from that gloomy forsaken place, it had a weird unearthly sound like boggarts were said to make at night in the lane by the graveyard at Heights Church. But on dark nights the turning wheel filled the empty rooms and the adjacent fields with the loudest and most terrifying groans that ever struck a human ear. It seemed as if the old black mill were racked with pain and writhing and groaning in an agony that would bring its walls down in ruins. In going to and from the school I used to stand about a hundred yards away till I had heard the wheel turn, but on windy nights I was sometimes caught near it, and I ran for my life, for I thought the groanings were hellish boggarts that were rushing after me and trying to clutch my coat in the darkness. I hated to go to that school and was glad when it closed for want of scholars.

EARLY MILL LIFE

When I began to work half-time, I went to school in the village, till I became a full time worker. I was a piecer with my mother and one day before I had been passed for full time an inspector came to the mill and I was hid and half smothered in a bag of shoddy. Trailing wearily about a mulegate all day took the sunshine out of my young life, and I grew depressed about it. No loitering through the summer meadows going to Castleshaw school, and no playing truant on the moor in wimberry time. No climbing the wall in Waters Lane every morning to watch the trout flash into the culvert under the road. The mill windows were plain glass, and from the mulegate I could see all the valley, the lanes, cottages and farmsteads up to the dark steep of Friarmere moor. In summer if the windows had been frosted glass, I should have felt less keenly the wearying grind of my toil, and in the haytime, how I longed to be in the meadows. To my young mind there seemed to be something wrong in the scheme of things, that made what our parson called "God's children" toil in stuffy mill rooms all day, while cows could lie in the sunny fields. In winter it felt less hard for I had shelter in rough weather, but the room was cold and my fingers so numb that I could scarcely piece a broken thread. There was a little fireplace at one end of the room that held about a handful of slack coal. The mill was turned by the joint power of a little steam engine and a waterwheel. There were three sets of carding machines and three self acting mules, and in the basement room there was the finishing plant. The finished goods were women's shawls made from shoddy and cotton. A cottage woman had two shawls, one for everyday wear, and a better shawl for Saturdays and Sundays. In winter the mill was lit by paraffin lamps hung on wires that were stretched across the rooms, and every afternoon a man went round and filled the lamps with oil. In his young days my father had worked at a mill where candles lit the rooms as described in "The Watermill". We had two masters at the mill, father and son, and the father always said that no working man was worth more than a pound a week, no matter how skilled he was, or how important the work he had to do. One man was carder, engineer and firebeater for a pound a week, and sometimes when busy in the cardroom, he forgot the boiler fire till it was nearly out, and then he had to slave and toil to get the steam up again as the waterwheel could not turn the machines. How he used to rush down the steps to the boiler house with his waistcoat open and his hair flying in the wind.

The spinning was piecework, and my father's wages rarely reached a pound a week, and there were weeks when the work was so bad that when he had paid his piecers their wages, he had two shillings left for himself. At such times my brother and I had oatmeal porridge from Monday to Saturday. Some days we had a spoonful of treacle with it, other days milk, and occasionally a cup of home brewed ale. It is called a healthy food "rough and enough", but it went down badly every day in the week.

One of the blackest memories of my early years is of a Christmas time. About the middle of December there came one of the roughest storms of the year with a high wind that filled the lanes with snow level to the wall tops. Huge drifts were piled over the hedges and against the walls and doors of the houses. Work at the mill had been bad for over a month, and we were never worse poverty stricken. We had no paraffin for our lamp and barely a barrowful of coal. If a neighbour woman had come into our house on that Christmas eve, she would have seen a father, mother and two little lads sitting in silence and gloom as they watched a few red cinders die down in the grate. We knew that in the neighbour houses there were great warm fires, carol singing and Christmas cakes and puddings. Our dinner on that freezing Christmas day was a plate of porridge and a spoonful of treacle. So my early working years dragged on, but I had begun to write rhymes, and found it a pleasure. We were not the only family that sat at a bare table. I remember a family who had a boy, and one day they had a luxury dinner, a potato pie, and the boy said, "mi fayther had o' th' beef, and mi mother an' eaur Jane an' me had o' th' potatoes". One day a man brought a pie in a dish to be warmed on the mill boiler for his dinner, and when he took off the crust, there was meal porridge under it. They say it's a long road that's never a turning, and at last better days came to us. My father became head spinner at another mill where the master was a gentleman, and the spinning was all wool with scarcely a broken thread in an hour. My brother and I went with him, and happily my mother's working days were over. In later life I could not forget how every Friday night in winter and often in rough weather, I had gone with my mother to a grocer's shop in the village and stood, never less than an hour, in a corner as far away as we could get from the other customers. My mother kept missing her turn to be served, as she had not enough money to pay for what we required. The shop woman would now and then look towards us and motion my mother to go to the counter, but she shook her head and turned away. It was cold standing on the bare stone flags at the far end of the shop and it hurt me to see her shivering under her shawl. At last when no more customers came in she got served, and it was late when we went up the dark Castleshaw valley with no words spoken on the way. I hated Friday night, and I knew my mother dreaded it. Shy and sensitive,

CASTLESHAW SCHOOL

she was pained and distressed by having to go into debt, and in thinking that the other customers knew about it, and they did know, but every penny we owed was paid when we had got from under the heels of the bully and his father.

HANDLOOM WEAVING

There were no looms at the mill; all the weaving was done at the hillside farms and cottages, and chiefly in the bed rooms. I heard a millowner say that when he went round the hillside houses of his weavers to take stock at Christmas, he had to stride over people in their beds. Before the warps left the mill they were run through a solution of size, and then taken out into a field and stretched over long sticks and hurdles to dry. At Far Hey my father and other neighbour weavers sized their warps at home. In bad weather a warp was wrapped round the breadrail to be dried by the fire, and it always gave the house a greasy unpleasant smell. When the threads of a warp were tender they were said to "breyk an' never speyk", or break without the weaver knowing. If a warp was found to be too damp when placed in the loom, a bucket pierced with holes and filled with hot cinders was placed under it. A weaver living at a distance had generally a donkey to carry his woven piece to the mill, and when he had received his wages it was called "bunting", and sometimes on his way home he would call at an alehouse and stay for days till he had spent every penny of the "bunting brass". He would then load his donkey and reach home full of ale and penitence, where sat like Tam o' Shanter's wife his

> "sulky sullen dame
> gathering her brows like a gathering storm
> nursing her wrath to keep it warm".

As a lad I saw warps and sacks of weft piled up in the lobby at the Royal Oak Inn, Heights, when the weavers were spreeing, and their donkeys grazing in the inn field. All weavers were not spenders. I knew one man who was said to be as "greedy as sin" for work. He got out of bed in the morning into his

33

loomgate, and out of it into bed at night. In weaving at home men were not tied to remain at their work like people who worked in the mills, and many cottage looms were idle on hunting days, and the weavers long linsey aprons could be seen blowing in the wind on the hilltops. When a loom chamber was lit up at midnight, the weaver had been hunting and was making up lost time. Joe o' Breb's always said that his loom knew when the hounds were out, and it would not work. The shuttle wouldn't run, the "yelds" kept sticking, and the wheels and weights conspired together to make him go hunting. Some men would have cured it, but Joe didn't, he put his coat on and went out singing.

> "I love a lass, a pipe and a glass
> Gaily along life's road I pass,
> Jolly and free, it just suits me,
> Out with hounds in the morning".

Joe's lines fit a light heart, and a light foot, and gaily I have sung them when striding through bracken and moorgrass to Black Moss reservoir. I believe Joe gave me the funeral card to a famous Saddleworth huntsman.

> To the Memory of the late
> Mr. John Mallalieu,
> Of the Cross Keys Inn, Saddleworth
> Church, who for fifty years was a keen
> hunter, and for twelve years huntsman
> of the Saddleworth Harriers.
> Died July 5th, 1868,
> In the 66th year of his age.
> And was interred at Saddleworth
> on the 10th inst.
> John Mallalieu was laid in his grave
> with a brown churchside hare on his
> coffin, so that in death he would be
> near something that he had loved
> in life.

When we lived at Millcroft, I remember how gladly I went with another lad to Black Moss Reservoir where we had been told that wild ducks were nesting and we could get their eggs. I took one of my mother's baskets and told her that I would bring it back full of eggs and have one to my breakfast in the morning. When we reached the reservoir there were ducks on the water and we searched among the grass for hours, and found nothing but empty nests. We thought someone must have been there before us, and going sadly homewards we met a man on the catchwater and he told us the birds were seagulls and their eggs not fit to eat.

GUN AND WILD BIRDS

My father wanted me to learn moorcraft and how to charge and handle a muzzle loading gun, but I loved wild birds too well to ever think of shooting them. What really made me make a dead set against it was something I saw one Saturday afternoon in June. There was a fresh wind blowing up the valley and I stood on the embankment of a mill dam watching martins flying over the water. How fast they flew, weaving in and out, twisting and twirling, rising and dipping, as if they were trying to excel each other in evolutions of flight, and how they seemed to be enjoying it. Bill o' J's came on the embankment with his gun, and I knew that it meant death to those little birds, for he was matched to shoot against another man, and the martins were his practice birds. With his gun ready, he waited till one made a driving shot like a pigeon from a trap, and cursing him under my breath, I went to the other end of the dam. I could see the white breasts of the little birds tossing among the waves as they were being washed to where I stood, and as I lifted them out of the water I felt an intense loathing for their slayer. They had nests and young in the corners of the mill windows, and I went home over the fields saying to myself I will never shoot at a wild bird, and I have kept my word. Yet in August and September I loved to go with my father on the moor when he stood the "crow" and tried to call birds with a hazel pipe or peg. His pegs were about the length and thickness of a lead pencil, and when he had bored the pith out of them they were placed on the mantelpiece to dry, and if one cracked it was useless.   Other moormen did without pegs, but my father always said that a call given through a peg carried farther than one given by the mouth alone.   I always lay in a hollow with a setter dog at my side.   I remember one morning when it was still dark he was giving the hen call and a cock came whirring and dropped on his boot.   The most beautiful sights that I have seen were early mornings and late evenings on the moors.   Mornings when the sun was newly risen and its first beam swept towards us like the incoming tide of a hazy golden sea.   It marked the end of the "crow", and then a light wind would blow up and whirl the white haze about in a frolic making the moor play hide and seek under it.   Evenings, when unseen hands seemed to be ever changing the shapes and colours of the clouds as they drifted towards the sunset and the black smoke of Lancashire towns. What a peace came to the moor at dusk with only one sound that neither day nor night can hush, the sound of waters splashing down stony cloughs.   On one of these evenings when the harvest moon was up over the far away hills, we went along the moortop to a road and called at an inn.   It was the first time that I had been in one, and I felt half afraid of the big moorland men who sat round the tables with their pots of ale, for I thought they were the highwaymen of Blackstone Edge that I had heard my mother talk about.   But there came a time when I grew to seek and love their company, and I got from old characters in mooredge inns some of the folk tales that are found in my books.

OLD SONGS OF THE INNS

We often went off the moor in the evening to one or other of the inns, and those hours are unforgetable.   There is a lamp hung in my memory that lights up a room, and I see a little speer or ceiling where I used to sit.   The floor was yellow sanded and the walls were blue limewashed like we had at home.   The long tables had been scrubbed almost to whiteness, and the nail heads shone like bits of silver. The fire was built of peat, and plain well worn seating went round the room.   On one side wall there was a coloured print of Lord Nelson and on the other side a long flitch of bacon. The company were hillmen, farmers and handloom weavers, men without sham or veneer, plain and strong as their own Pennine country, that is still called the backbone of England. They had been born and reared on it, and its rugged strength could be seen in their limbs and weathered faces.

At that time my father had a good round tenor voice and was always ready to set a night of song going at an inn. How widely the songs I heard on those nights differ from the songs I now hear in country inns. There were no "Toosy Woosy, she is sweet as sugar candy" songs on those nights. The songs those men sang and loved to hear were chiefly of battle, adventure, poaching and hunting, and the chorus singing was like a pack of hounds in full cry. If my father had a brace of grouse in his pocket he was in high spirits and his first song was :

> "Now westlin winds and slaughtering guns
> Bring Autumn's pleasant weather,
> The moorcock springs on whirring wings
> Among the blooming heather".

A Shepherd always sang "The Battle of the Nile" with the ponderous opening line :

> "In the year one thousand seven hundred and ninety eight",

and ending with

> "British sailors fought like lions at the battle of the Nile".

His second song was "The Battle of Trafalgar".

> "On the twenty first of October at the rising of the sun,
> We formed our line of action and at twelve o'clock begun,
> Lord Nelson to his men did say, the Lord will help us on this day,
> Fire away my brave British boys".

One poaching song came from Lincolnshire with the chorus,

> "It's my delight on a shiny night
> In the season of the year".

Another was "Bill Brown".

> "Come all ye lads of high renown,
> That love to drink good ale that's brown,
> And pull the lofty pheasants down,
> With powder, shot and gun".

Another song of Nottinghamshire.

> "In Thornimore woods in Nottinghamshire,
> Ri fol laro laro laddie di,
> In Robin Hood's bold Nottinghamshire,
> Ri fol laro laro laddie di".

I never think of that song but it makes me recall a lovely morning in the meadows near Hollingworth. I went along singing it blithely to myself when a young woman came from a side path and said with a laugh "A penny for your song". I was tongue tied for a moment but recovering myself I said, "I'll sell both song and singer for three halfpence", holding my hand out for the money. "Not of my money" she said. "Well" I said, "Give me a penny for the song and I will throw the singer in for nothing". "You might be dear as a gift" she said, "A light heart and a light head go together".

I was heart whole then, and I thought she was the bonniest young woman I had ever seen. I have wondered what life had in store for her on that sunny June morning. She may have known its ups and downs, mothered many children and become a sad faced careworn old woman. Who said a man should have a new wife every spring and did Balzac hate a woman with thick ankles ? Had he been with me in Hollingworth meadows on that morning he would have seen ankles to dream about.

Hunting songs were among the most rousing and one "Squire Firth of Bank Hall" in Derbyshire, tells about a fox that ran forty miles.

"Near forty long miles this old traitor did run
Till he earthed in Cloud Valley near Congleton".

A favourite was "The White Hare of Macclesfield".

"It was near to Macclesfield town my boys,
As I have heard them tell,
There once was a white hare
That used for to dwell.
It was the Squire Stansfield
A hearing of the news,
Says he "I'll catch this white hare
Any day I choose".

A song said to have come from Warwickshire, with the chorus,

"We'll all go a hunting today
All nature is balmy and gay
So we'll join the glad throng
That goes laughing along
And we'll all go a hunting today".

"Old Towler" was a favourite and "Brave Thomas Kaye" a song made at Holmfirth in Yorkshire was often sung,

"On the thirtieth of October just by break of day
To Ramsden in Cartworth came brave Thomas Kaye".

The highwayman songs were "Brannon on the Moor" and the "Highwaymen of Blackstone Edge"

"It's of a fearless highwayman a story I will tell,
His name was William Brannan and in Ireland he did
dwell,
It was on the Wicklow Mountains he began his wild
career,
And many a wealthy gentleman before him shook with
fear.

39

Chorus—Brannan on the moor, Brannan on the moor,
        Boldhearted and undaunted stood young Brannan on
        the moor.

    A brace of loaded pistols true he carried night and day
    He never robbed the poor man on the king's highway,
    And what he'd taken from the rich, like Turpin and
        Black Bess,
    He always did divide with the widow in distress".

The above are two of the seven verses. I heard a poacher sing the Blackstone Edge song several times, and I do not think what it describes ever happened on that moorland road. If it did it was like what happened in another part of England where three highwaymen stripped three gentlemen stark naked in the presence of their ladies, and a song was made of it called "The Stark Naked Robbery". The poacher who was called Jack, had a brother who was heir to a bit of property and he kept saying to Jack, "Theau sees it goes bi heirship". Having heard it repeated till he was weary Jack knocked his brother off an alehouse form and shaking his fist said, "Sithi this goes by steaum, everything doesn't go bi heirship".

"The White Cockade" was a good chorus song.

    "It was on a Monday morning as I walked o'er yon moss,
    I had no thought of listing till a soldier I did cross,
    He kindly did invite me to drink the flowing bowl,
    He advanced, he advanced, he advanced five guineas and
        a crown.

    They say my love has listed and wears a white cockade,
    He is a handsome young man besides a roving blade,
    He is a handsome young man, and he's gone to serve the
        king,
    Oh my very, Oh my very, Oh my very heart lies breaking
        all for the love of him.

Oh may he never prosper, and may he never thrive,
With anything he takes in hand as long as he's alive,
May the very ground he treads upon, the grass refuse to
grow,
Since he's been, Since he's been, since he's been the
cause of my sorrow, grief and woe".

One of the few love songs was "Chloe" a shepherd's song.

"Arise my dear Chloe, it is all a broad day,
If we tarry much longer our flocks they will stray".

The tune is low, sweet and sighing like a little wind in
a rose garden. A man was singing that song in a village inn with
his eyes closed and another man threw a glass of ale in the singer's
face and said "Oppen thi een, aw dunnot like to yer blind songs".
There was a tall handloom weaver who wore his grey linsey apron
on Sundays and his wife said "He'd rayther go beawt breeches
nur beawt his apron". He always sang the same two songs and
coming as they usually did, after the thunder of battle songs they
seemed like sunshine streaming into the room. Before he had
sung four lines of "Jockey to the Fair" the faces of the farmers
were lit with smiles, and their feet tapping to the tune on the
floor. I think if a man had two left legs the tune would put
dancing into them.

"Twas on a bright and sweet May day,
When nature painted all things gay,
Taught larks to sing and lambs to play
And decked the meadows fair.
Young Jockey early in the morn
Arose and tripped it o'er the lawn,
His Sunday coat the youth put on,
For Jenny had vowed away to run
With Jockey to the Fair, the Fair,
With Jockey to the Fair".

I have seen queries in newspapers from people who
wished to know who had written the words and tune of the song,

41

and though I have looked for replies, I have yet to see one. It maybe that some young happy poet wandering up a green valley on a May morning caught the tune from a skylark's song and sat down among wild flowers and wrote words to it. There is so much joyousness of youth and springtime in the song that it could not have been written among streeted houses. After a day's flint hunting I have sung "Jockey to the Fair" at night along the lonely moorland roads and it always set my feet tripping to the tune and shortened the miles.

The weaver's second song was an old ballad "The Banks of Sweet Dundee", and he always sang it well. Here are three verses.

"It is of a farmer's daughter so beautiful I'm told
Her parents died and left her five hundred pounds in gold,
She lived with a rich uncle the cause of all her woe,
But you shall hear this maiden fair did prove his over-
throw.

Her uncle had a ploughboy that Mary loved full well
Down in her uncle's garden their tales of love did tell,
It chanced there was a rich squire who oft came her to see
But Mary loved the ploughboy on the Banks of Sweet
Dundee.

It was on a summer's morning her uncle went straightway,
And knocked at Mary's bedroom door and unto her did
say,
Come rise my pretty maiden, a lady you may be
The squire is waiting for you on the Banks of Sweet
Dundee".

After the pressgang had been bribed and taken the plough-boy to sea, Mary shot her uncle and the squire.

Of all the songs that I heard my father sing there were two verses of "The Waggoner" which made me see pictures that have never faded. There is a magical something in them that seems to hold much of the sunshine of my boyhood and stirs me as it did when I sat by the hearth at Millcroft.

> "Now summer it has come.
> What pleasure there will be,
> The small birds are singing
> Upon every green tree".

In those four lines simple as they are, I see all that my boyhood loved in the Castleshaw valley, as it was before the reservoirs were made, every bend and curve of the brook, the old stone bridges, the fields, meadows, mills and cottages that are gone, and will never be seen again. The other verse is,

> "Now Michaelmas has come,
> What pleasure we shall find,
> We'll make the gold to fly
> Like chaff before the wind.
> And every lad shall take his lass
> And set her on his knee
> Singing wo my lads sing wo".

If that verse does not reveal a picture of bygone merry England I do not know where to look for one. At bedtime on summer nights I have sung it to myself as I stood at my window looking out on the dim hilly fields. There was ever something in those joyous words that I found more pleasant than old wine to lie down with and give me a good night's rest. It seems strange that in my boyhood I never heard anyone sing the famous "Holmfirth Anthem", nor can I remember hearing the no less famous "A Bright Rosy Morning" a song so full of hunting ecstacy that it seems to carry a horn and wear a scarlet coat if ever a song did.

I sometimes think that if I wandered far enough along the old hilly lanes of the Pennines I should have the luck to find an old inn like those I knew in my boyhood. A motherly inn with the warm heart of old England still beating under its oak beams.

One with an old fashioned kitchen, with lime washed walls and sanded floor, oak panelled langsettle, rush seated chairs with spindled backs, grandfather's clock with a moon dial, oak corner cupboard. I breadfleck hung with oatcakes and bunches of herbs, and a coffee mill, brass candlesticks and Robin Hood and Little John in coloured pottery on the mantlepiece, and perhaps funeral cards in black frames on the walls. In the taproom I might find moorend men who would sing the old songs that I am longing to hear.

"The Spade".

"Give me the spade and the man that can use it
A fig for the lord with his soft silken hand,
Let the man that has strength never stoop to abuse it".

"A Life on the Ocean Wave" and other songs that I have not heard for many years.

We have still a few old inns that look so homely and welcoming that it is hard to pass them in closed daytime hours. Yet how often I have had a drink in those hours, and said hell to the law and the lawgivers. Some of our old country inns have been gutted and given fine interiors. Others have had their outside walls plastered with a veneer called stucco, that hides the warm time mellowed stone, and gives them sham faces. A few have been demolished and swagger inns built on their sites. They are foreigners out of harmony with the green countryside and the moors. They seem to stare brazenly at the homely wayfarer and are not for roadmenders and other working folks. They are really town inns, and the callers who come in their cars.

A BRUSH STEYL WEDDING.

One evening I went off the moor to a roadside inn that is now closed and I saw what people called "a brush steyl wedding". There were five or six local men in the taproom and two strangers, a man and a woman on a seat near the window. They had their heads together and were whispering to each other.

44

The landlord said they had met casually in front of his house and he was going to marry them over the brush steyl. He went into the kitchen and came back covered from head to foot with a white gown like a parson's surplice. It was his wife's nightdress. He had a book in one hand and a long handled sweeping brush in the other. He asked the strangers if they were ready and the man said yes. When they got up I thought they seemed to be about middle age and looked more respectable than most tramps that I had seen pass along that road. Their faces were clean and so were their clothes. Two men came out from behind a table and took hold of the brush, one at each end, and the landlord placed the pair near the taproom door and told the woman to jump over the extended brush that was held about a half a yard above the flagged floor. When they had both jumped over it the landlord read something out of a book and placed a ring on the woman's finger and it fell off on to the floor. It was the ring he used at such weddings. The woman asked him if they were properly wed and he said yes, it was the custom of the country. The landlady brought us a pitcher full of ale, and we wished them long life and prosperity. They thanked us and the landlord told them to go into the kitchen and get something to eat. When we left the inn at moonrise, I looked up the road towards the moors, and saw two dim figures walking side by side as they faded into the haze of that lovely August night. I remember that some years afterwards two locals were married over the brush steyl at the Royal Oak inn, Heights, but I do not think they lived together.

WRITING RHYMES.

I wrote rhymes in my early days unknown to my father, for I thought if he knew there would be an end to it. I had to take my mother into my secret for she had to supply me with paper. The only plain white paper we had in the house was that in which her groceries were wrapped and it was badly creased, and had to be smoothed out with her clothes iron. When I ran short I had to wait till she had been to the shop again. I dared not read my verses to her when my father was in the house for I thought he would regard it as a hindrance to my learning moorcraft, but one day in the dog hunting season he caught me stringing some lines together. I was terribly afraid for I felt sure he would tear them up, but to my surprise and delight, he said that if I would write six four line verses about a laneside well he would give me three-pence on the Saturday. My mother gave a piece of shop paper an extra ironing and on Saturday noon when I gave him my lines, he put his hand into his pocket and gave me three pennies. It was a sunny day in summer and I have a vivid recollection of jumping over a wall into a field and trying to fly. Three pennies were all the money I possessed and I rubbed them with oil at the mill till they shone like gold.

With no opposition at home I felt that I must have a desk, and the scourer at the mill gave me a few pieces of wood from an old soap box, and with bits of greasy leather, my father's saw, a few tacks and a hammer I knocked one together. It was not a Sheraton, either in design or workmanship, but having regard to the high purpose to which it was to be put, I thought it worthy of a place among our furnishings, but my mother thought the opposite, and I had to keep it on a shelf in the coal cote. On summer evenings to get away from the other lads, I carried my desk across a field to the shelter of a blackberry hedge, and scribbed away till dusk. My verses were written with a stump of a lead pencil, and as they soon faded on the coarse paper my mother used them to light the fire. One Saturday I walked with her over the hills to Oldham, where she bought me a new pencil and a little desk made of strong papiermache, and I remember how proudly I carried it the six miles to Millcroft. It was a dark green colour and it looked well on the top of our oak chest. To keep me supplied with paper she bought me a few sheets from a grocer's shop, and as they were clean and not creased I reserved them for what I called my best poems.

About this time I saw a few lines from Goldsmith's "Deserted Village". It was like seeing a light from heaven that I had not seen before, and I would have given the clothes off my back for the complete poem. "Sweet auburn, loveliest village of the plain". All day long I kept repeating the lines I knew, and got cursed at the mill for losing myself and allowing my "ends" or broken threads to run down in the mulegate. A few weeks had gone when I saw "The Works of Oliver Goldsmith" among other books in a newsagent's window at the village. There were also Shakespeare, Walter Scott, Longfellow, Cowper and other poets that I had not heard about, all bound in yellow paper covers and published by John Dicks, London. The price of Goldsmith's Works was ninepence, and I thought my mother might lend me sixpence, but I did not ask her for just then work at the mill was so bad that our joint wages were barely sufficient to provide food, fire and rent. We paid three shillings and sixpence a week for a living room, small kitchen and two bedrooms. I had not spent the threepence my father had given me and how to make it into ninepence was beyond my thinking and scheming. I had a miserable time for it seemed certain that someone would buy the book before I had saved the money. Almost every night in the week I hurried home from the mill, bolted my porridge, and ran to the village sometimes in the rain, to see if the book was still in the window. I had about a mile to run, but I would have run two rather than gone uneasy to bed about it. If people went into the shop while I stood outside wet and shivering, I thought they were going for the book, and always glad when they came out with it still in the window.

I had fivepence when disaster overtook me in cutting off my only source of revenue. John Milnes who owned Millcroft and the farmlands carried on the business of a cloth merchant, and in the evening he sometimes gave me a penny for taking his letters to the post in the village. One summer evening going down the brook side with the letters in my hand, I saw a large trout floundering in the water. It had probably taken a dose of dye water and I knelt down and waited for it to come to my side of the brook. It came close to the grassy edge and I shot my hands into the water, missed the trout and the letters went floating down towards a deep weir pool. It was a fat red spotted beauty and no wonder that it made me forget the letters. I ran to the hedge for a stick and managed to rake them out of the water before they reached the weir. They were soaked and stuck together in my hand with the water seeping through my fingers, the ink had run and the addresses were blurred and unreadable, and my mind was blurred with wondering what to do. I dared not go back to Mr. Milnes, so I went slowly to the village and when the post had gone I pushed the letters into the box. Mr. Milnes said nothing about it, but he never sent me again to the post. A penny now and then was something, and the loss of it might mean that I should not get the book. I worried about it, and the haytime found me ill and away from work. I sat by the fire white as a ghost and weak as a kitten, and the neighbours did not make me any better by saying the gravedigger was shaking his spade in my face. One Saturday noon when my mother had brushed her clogs and donned her weekend shawl to go to the village, I said, "Mother here is fivepence and I want you to lend me fourpence and bring me a book from the newsagent's. I have written the title and the price on this slip of paper". She told me to stay in the house, but when she had gone I went out and lay in the sun against a grassy hedge, watching the haymakers. What a long time she seemed to be away, and I began to think that the book had been sold which made me feel worse than ever. At last I saw her coming up the valley and stole back into the house, and I cannot remember ever longing for anything as I longed for that book, nor have I felt a greater joy than I did when she took it out of her basket. In a few weeks I had committed "The Deserted Village" to memory and tried to write a poem like it, only to fail and go back to lyrics like the Wayside Well and other poems.

A neighbour lady lent me a book that contained a few recitations from Shakespeare, and it made me long for the yellow backed book that was still in the newsagent's window, but I had no money, not even a penny. It was the village fair, and my mother usually gave my brother and I a penny each, and I was surprised

EMILY WRIGLEY

AMMON WRIGLEY

when she gave us twopence each. I did not spend mine, and most of the afternoon I lingered about the newsagent's window wishing that I had a shilling. They say one door never shuts but another opens, and I began to run errands to the village for the neighbours, to a hilltop farm for pills, and to an alehouse for yeast for baking and home brewing. Sometimes I went to a handloom weaver's house for bobbins of thread and balls of worsted, and he had always to root among his greasy mill bobbins to find what I wanted. When he had no warp in his loom he hawked smallware about the hillside houses, and always wore a tall silk hat and a long faded black coat. I got a penny for doing the errands and when I had saved a shilling I ran home one Saturday with the Shakespeare in my hand. I learned Othello's Defence, and other pieces, and recited them aloud at night, but had I known what was coming I would not have recited a line when my father was in the house. It became bad enough for me, but worse for my mother.

RECITING

My father was proud of my reciting and talked about it in the inns and when he came home on a Saturday night he brought three or four of his moor friends to drink our home brewed ale and hear me recite. It was always near midnight when they came and I had gone to bed. Then my mother had to come into my room and shake me out of my sleep. I got up without disturbing my younger brother and followed her down the stair rubbing my sleepy eyes open. Then I stood on the carpet of clean washed sacking in nothing but my shirt and began "Friends, Romans, Countrymen", or if it was "Othello's Defence" "Most potent grave and reverend signiors". On a Saturday night when my mother had done her weekly "siding up" the house was as clean as the doorstep of heaven and it pained me to see the careless brutes smoking and spitting on the fender and the hearthstone. My mother protested, but they took no notice of her, and when I began to shiver she sent me to bed. I wonder if Shakespeare was ever recited to men who knew less about him, and I am certain that they did not know what the recitals were about. They were

D

men who had been brought up roughly on the mooredge, and knew little about manners or decency. One was a notorious poacher on all the local moors, and the man who sat next to him always said that I should have to be a parson.

CATCHING SPARROWS

At the Wakes time and the backend of the year there were sparrow shoots at the country inns, and I had to go with my father and other men at night to net sparrows in the ivied walls of houses. Very often no permission had been obtained and we had to wait till the lights were out and the inmates in bed. Then the large net was fastened at each side of two long light poles and reared against the house wall as silently as possible and the sparrows flushed into it. My duty was to watch the house and give the alarm if I saw or heard anything, and a few times when trespassing in gardens, doors opened and we had to race away without sparrows.

We left Millcroft and went to live near the village and in one way my life changed for the worse. I began to mate with village lads who had gone to the same school and I soon found that idling about the streets was not like wandering alone by the streams and among the fields and moors of the Castleshaw valley. At first my mates called me The Dreamer, because I talked about books and it led me to throw reading and verse writing to the winds. I was fairly fleet of foot, and my mates urged me to take up running. I won a few jumping matches against village lads and then entered the youths race at sports in Greenfield.

I had a large following of trainers and backers, and no lad ever had a more remarkable preparation for a race. One fine evening I ran a trial against the watch, though neither I nor any of my backers knew what was good time for the hundred yards. My running costume consisted of an old pair of cricket drawers cut off above the knee. They were a man's size, so were my pumps that were tied to my feet with yards of string. There were about thirty lads present when the hundred yards had been measured out, and I had to start at the drop of a cap while my pacemakers ran in their stockinged feet. We had only one watch and it was held at the finish. I ran well till one of my pumps came off, but I managed to finish in eight seconds dead. My backers conferred together and after a lot of whispering the trial was declared unsatisfactory and one of them kicked me and said that I had never tried to run. My pumps were tied on again for another trial, and running full of fire like a little steam engine I did the distance in what the timekeeper said was a shade under seven seconds. My backers conferred again and agreed that the time was fairly good considering that the grass was nearly up to my knees. I can see that watch now, it was large and round like a potatoe and of a dull brassy colour. The lad who owned it said there were wheels inside, but he would not let us look for fear we might spoil them.

On Whit-Saturday noon I left Delph for Greenfield with a following of backers and trainers like a Whitsuntide procession. I began to strip an hour before my heat was to be run, for it took my trainers a long time to gear me up, and the other competitors had a rare laugh at my costume. I had got a pair of pumps to fit my feet, and one of my trainers had a quart bottle full of cold tea that he said was to keep me cool, and I had to drink a pint just before I ran my heat, which I won rather easily. I was compelled to drink the other pint of the nasty stuff on going to my mark for the final heat in which I got second place. It was a warm sunny day and going about the field I was surprised at the number of women who spoke to me about the beautiful whiteness of my shirt, and when I told my mother it pleased her. I have often wondered what would have happened to me if my trainers had told the other competitors that I had run a hundred yards in seven seconds.

A change came over me, I could not take to running, I longed for the trout streams, the green bracken and the high brown moor of Millstone Edge. I thought of my cousin Ammon Wrigley in the bleak windy graveyard at Heights Church. He was said to have been one of the most scholarly youths in the parish and died in his eighteenth year. So I had reading in my blood, and I went roaming over the moors and writing verse again. I joined the Mechanics Institute, and read poets that were new to me, Keats, Shelly, Tennyson and Burns. I taught myself to sketch from threepenny drawing books, and often went home on a Saturday noon, washed hands, and midnight found me at work copying some famous picture. From pencil I passed to pen and ink, and spent many happy Sundays on the moors with a sketch book.

I became interested in local history and antiquities, and one Saturday I had a short article in a local newspaper. The Mechanics Institute had then moved to a house that still stands opposite the bank. There was a smoke and conversation room in which the village wiseacres gathered at night and settled questions of national importance in a way that made the Government seem a lot of fools. Local news was discussed and dissected down to the most trivial detail, and if it concerned the shortcomings of some villager the dissection was merciless. My article passed through the dissecting operation with no destructive comment, but the full blast of the room's ridicule was turned on me personally. Among other things I was said to have copied every word of my article from an old book that no other member had seen, and on hearing this from a friend, I was afraid of going to the Institute. I kept away and published in the same newspaper several articles on local families. They were in parts racily written and served to put the wise men of the smoke room in their proper places. A Mutual Improvement Society was founded at the Institute and one night I went to a meeting with the intention of becoming a member, but the room reeked with the snobbish airs of a few well dressed members who were school teachers. One of them gave a reading, and in the after discussion a millworker said a few words and was promptly ridiculed by another scholastic gentlemen, and no one in mill clothes spoke again. We then waited for a young man who had promised to give a paper on Cromwell. I was astonished, for we worked together, and I knew that he could not write a paper on any subject, but he posed as a village somebody.

At last he bounced into the room and said "I am very sorry gentlemen, but I have not had time to write my paper about Mr. Oliver Cromwell, but I have been told that he was a very bad man, good night". I did not go to another meeting, and in a few weeks the class was dissolved as only the intellectual school teachers attended.

I began to give papers on local subjects before village societies and had about two discouraging experiences. I gave a paper at a school near Uppermill and as there was a good attendance, the committee invited me to give another paper at their next winter session. I consented and turned up on the appointed night to find five or six people in the room. I felt insulted and galloped through my paper, and waited for no vote of thanks, but hurried out of the room trying to kick myself for a fool. Some weeks later I met a man who had been present at that meeting and he said my paper was announced from the pulpit on the Sunday night, but some of the village saints had heard that I went into alehouses and they advised people to keep away. I had been wicked enough to pollute the pure teetotal air of the room with the smell of fourpenny ale and no doubt it would be thoroughly fumigated and then sweetened by the breaths of a few village saints and finally followed by a special purification service.

About this time I married Emily Hudson, a young woman from a hillside farm and got one of the best housewives in a parish famous for its clean, good fingered home loving women. We lived happily until her death in 1930, and I owe much to her helpfulness, for without it I could not have got through the writing I did at Beswicks and later at Hilltop.

FLINT HUNTING

From my boyhood I had been a roamer of the moors and about 1893 I began to search them for prehistoric remains in the form of flint implements. I was the first and for many years the only man in the parish to take up that kind of work, and early on I knew little about it, but an article by Robert Law of Todmorden, cleared away much that had been obscure. I never met him, but one evening I sat in the taproom at the Ram's Head inn, near Denshaw moor, while he and another man were at tea in the next room—I learned it after they had gone. I sometimes met George Marsden, the man who explored the prehistoric grave on Pule Hill. One glorious Whit-Saturday we crossed the Clowes Moor to March Hill and then called at the gamekeeper's house at Buckstones where I had to stand up and sing "Now westlin winds an' slaughtering guns". Our framed portraits as local pioneers are hung in the Tolson Memorial Hall, Huddersfield. I published a book about my flint hunting, and a handbook issued by the Halifax Museum Committee described it as "the best book that could be put into the hands of a beginner".

In those years I sometimes got lost on the moors. I was lost twice on the high ground above the treacherous swamps of Linsgreave. Once in November with a cold wind blowing from Blackstone Edge, I was about to go towards Dean Clough when I found that a fog had got round me. I had not noticed its approach, but I did not feel alarmed for the Huddersfield road was not far away and knowing that it would soon be dark I began to walk in what I thought was the right direction. I went on and on till I came to footprints in the peat. They were my own, I had walked in a circle and was lost. I wandered about till it grew dark and then I tried to set the moor on fire but the grass was too damp. Feeling as imprisoned as if I were within four thick walls, I sat down and lit my pipe. I had not been smoking very long before I began to nod and the pipe fell out of my mouth. Sleep meant death from exposure, so I got up and walked ten strides out and back again. About nine o'clock the wind rose to a gale and filled the night with a pack of furies that wailed and screamed over me as they were whirled away in the darkness. Having sat and walked alternately for about three hours, I began to shiver and fear that I could not last till daybreak. I had just got up to walk again when a furious gust nearly tore me off my feet, but to my great joy it swept the fog away and I could see the stars. I then found that the hellish noises were caused by the wind striking the Waystone, an isolated rock that stands on the high ridge of the moor. The stars gave me enough light to see my way to the Huddersfield road.

My third experience was on the moor beyond Wind Hills, where I got caught in the roughest storm of wind, rain and driving mist that I have ever known. I had no raincoat and was soon drenched to the skin. After I had wandered about for nearly an hour wading knee deep through sopping grass, I struck the stream that runs down through Whiteley Dean to Rakewood. I crossed it and went up the fields to Booth Hollins and down by the ruined Schofield Hall to Hollingworth Lake. I had then the long walk to Milnrow Station with a cold wet shirt sticking to my back. As I stood shivering on the platform waiting for a train, a lady came up to me and said, "You seem drenched, have you fallen in a brook".

"No" I replied "I have been caught in a rainstorm on the moors beyond Wind Hills".

"You'll get your death of cold, have you far to go" ?

"To Oldham" I said.

I stripped when I got home and took no harm. It is well to take a compass when going over the moors in winter or in unsettled weather. When lost in a fog follow the first little stream and it will lead you to a larger stream that will take you down to farmlands. I have known men to be found dead on the moors who had crossed several streams that would have taken them down to fields and meadows, but they had not the sense to follow one. I think one would feel justified in setting the moor afire when lost in a fog. One must keep warm.

HOW FLINT GOT ON TO THE MOORS

I remember one Sunday when crossing the moor from Cupwith to Higher Green Owlers, I met a shepherd with two dogs at his heels. It was easy to see that he was a true son of the moor, one who had been cradled in heather. From continually tramping over rough ground he had acquired the moorman's walk, a rolling up and down gait, a kind of pitching like a boat on a rough sea. He was like most moormen, ruggedly built, with plenty of bone in his frame, and as weather-beaten as the rocks on Blacker Edge. From long association, the moor had grown into him from head to foot, giving him that fresh breeziness of personality which invariably makes a moorman an interesting companion. He had spent, as I knew, a lifetime wrestling with wind and weather on those bleak, pitiless heights, and, I believe, if the law had compelled him to doff his shepherd garments to don a silk hat and a frock coat, he would have pined away in three weeks.

He pulled out a short, discoloured clay pipe, and began to fumble in his pockets :

"Hasto a match" ? he asked.

"A match ? yes, take a few", I replied handing him a box.

When he had lit his pipe, he said :

"A bit o' bacca, mon, is like meyt un drink sometimes".

"I prefer a rasher of ham and two eggs just now" I replied, for I had tramped from Linsgreave over Waystone Edge that afternoon, and was about as hungry as the proverbial hunter.

"Theau' bin gettin flints, aw guess" ? he queried.

"A few".

"Toh breyk op for th' hens" ?

"Not exactly".

"Wot for then" ?

"Because they are relics of primitive man".

"Um", he grunted, obviously mystified by my reply.

"Yes", I went on, triumphantly, and with the intention of mystifying him still further, "The flints in my pocket belong to the Bronze Age, and probably also the Neolithic Age".

"O ay", he replied adding, "Aw think ut theau belungs to thoose lot, too, doesn't toh" ?

I laughed at this sally, and said "probably".

"Theau favvers um a bit, for sure".

I lit my pipe and made no reply. Then he went on :

"There's a lot o leatheryeds ut comes peylin op here after flints, ut hasn't wit thi wur born wi".

"How's that" ? I asked.

"Heaw's that" ? he began, with the emphasis of the man who knows, "Thoose flints ut theau's bin samming up wur browt op here bi a lot a young devuls o setting th' moor a-foire afore ther wur ony matches".

"How can that be" ? I said, feeling certain that I had a poser for him, "when flints are never found in the peat, but always on the hard ground under it".

He looked at me, pitying my ignorance, then he said, "It's this road, dusto see. Flint is so sharp ut its hetten through th' turf on to the hard rock".

"That sounds very strange" I replied.

"Ay, but it's reet, lad".

We filled our pipes again, and I bade him good afternoon.

NEW FRIENDS

About 1895 I made two new friends who were unlike any that I had previously known. One was Mr. Morgan Brierley, a member of the Manchester Literary Club, and a gentleman who had written much on many subjects. He was widely and deeply read in classical literature, and the hours I spent in his study at Denshaw House are among my most treasured memories. Unhappily our friendship ended all too soon, for he died in 1897, and in 1900 his daughter Helen Brierley published a charming memoir of her father with selections from his writings. The other friend was Mr. G. F. Buckley of Linfitts House. He was a bachelor and well read in history and archaeology, and a member of the Yorkshire Archaeological Society, and also of the Lancashire and Cheshire Society. A long shelf in his sitting room was filled with the Transactions of both Societies. If I did not go over to his house two or three nights in a week, he would send the gardener or coachman to see what I had been doing. The people of his own district spoke of him as "A fine old English gentleman, one of the olden time". I often saw a bowl nearly full of pennies in a corner of the kitchen window, and one of the servants told me that they were for beggars and other callers who passed along the road. Yet he was the chairman of the local bench of magistrates and the other members were trying to suppress begging.

THE ROMAN FORT AT CASTLESHAW

When we talked about the local Roman fort he always said it was a myth and that he and other Saddleworth gentlemen had been over the site and seen nothing that agrees with the plan shown on the 1850 Ordnance Map. When I told him that I had seen the outlines of the fort from the hilly fields above Broadhead he said that I had imagined it, but I felt so certain about it that the brothers Schofield gave me permission to sink trial holes in the field on condition that I filled them up again. I could do little myself and I had to get the help of a few friends, and on Saturday October 9th 1897 we turned up fragments of Roman tiles and pottery, and there is no record of any earlier archaeological excavations on the site. The "finds" impressed Mr. Buckley and he leased the field from the Schofields, and in the summer of 1898 a number of trenches were dug that yielded more evidence of Roman occupation. On the 23rd of July, the Lancashire and Cheshire Society visited Castleshaw. It was a warm sunny day, and I am sure the old moorland hamlet had never seen so many fine and important ladies and gentlemen pass through it. In 1899 I had an article on the Castleshaw fort in the Yorkshire Post, and part of it appeared in The Antiquary and brought Sir John Barran and Mr. E. Kitson Clark from Leeds to see what had been explored. I met them by appointment and tried to get their Society to take up Mr. Buckley's work, but they said it was too near Lancashire.

At the beginning of his lease Mr. Buckley appealed to several local gentlemen to assist in exploring the most important historic site in the parish, but unbelievable as it may seem, he did not receive a single favourable reply.

After my article had appeared in the Yorkshire Post, Mr. Buckley began to take me to historic places and to meetings of the Lancashire Society in Manchester. I was not too happy on those occasions for they were attended by so many fine ladies and gentlemen that I felt ill at ease. He took me to Wilderspool, near Warrington, when the Lancashire and Cheshire Society visited that Roman station. It was a glorious day about midsummer, and a large company of ladies and gentlemen were on the field, all in light gay summer clothes, and as mine were shabby by contrast, I kept well in the background. When we got to Warrington a grand tea had been provided for us at the Town Hall. I did not wish to sit down with those fine folks and decided to dodge Mr. Buckley and get a sandwich with a glass of ale at an inn. I hid in a room upstairs, and was standing in front of a mirror busy combing my hair for about the fifteenth time and feeling glad that Mr. Buckley had not missed me when the door opened and he said "It takes you a long time to comb your hair". I was confused and could not speak for a moment; then I said "Yes, I cannot make it lie down", but it lay down of itself when I heard him speak. I followed him sheepishly into the tea room and he put me down between two ladies. The one on the right was about forty years of age and rather nice looking. She probably saw that I was unhappy and would like to be out of the room, so to put me at my ease she said, "What do you think about the station at Wilderspool".

"It seems more important than the one at Castleshaw in my country" I replied.

"Would you care to stay at my house for a week so that I could show you the historic places in the district" ?

"I work in the mill and could not get off" I replied.

I blundered through the tea for I had trouble with an unruly piece of chicken that insisted on wandering off my plate, and my knife and fork behaved badly in a tussle with a little bone. They could not strip it, and perhaps they had been used by a lady mayoress and resented the rude hands of a millworker. My clumsiness amused a lady on the other side of the table and it made my face burn like fire. After tea a gentleman told me that the lady who had spoken to me came from a hall in Shropshire. I did not go to see her.

RECEPTION

I went with Mr. Buckley to a reception at the City Art Gallery, Manchester. I had not the faintest notion what a reception was like and did not wish to go, but he would not take a refusal. At the Art Gallery we found a number of ladies and gentlemen inspecting some large beautiful pieces of decorated Roman Samian ware that had been found during excavations at Exchange Station. I thought this is the reception, and felt glad that I had come with Mr. Buckley for at that time I was greatly interested in Roman finds. We all went up a wide staircase and formed into a queue ; why I could not understand. At the head of it, I noticed two long green curtains and a man in a gold laced coat standing near them. I did not like the look of him, and wished I were in the street running to the Station. A gentleman at the head of the queue spoke to the gold laced man who then went through the curtains and shouted something that I could not make out. The gentleman and a lady then passed through the curtains, and this went on till Mr. Buckley went through them and left me wishing the floor would open and drop me into the room below. The flunkey had a shock when he saw me, but I had a greater shock. There I stood with a white cotton scarf round my neck and a cap in my hand.   He seemed to be wondering how has that ragamuffin got into the queue among ladies and gentlemen.   When he had looked me over from head to foot three or four times and I thought he was going to send for the police, he said snappishly, "What is your name".

"Ammon Wrigley" I replied weakly.

He passed through the curtains and shouted loud enough to be heard in Oldham "Mr. Ammon Rigby, ladies and gentlemen". "Mr. Rigby" then went into the room with all eyes on him, shook hands with a gentleman and slunk into a corner, where he had a stormy interview with himself.   That was my first and last reception.

THE IRON FURNACE NEAR CASTLESHAW,
1897 and 1907

At that time I wrote very little verse for I could not get rid of the antiquarian fever that I had caught at the Roman fort at Castleshaw, and it forced me to return to Cudworth and explore the mounds of iron scoria.   In 1907 I found and half explored the furnace in which the ore had been smelted.   Finding the work too heavy for me, I got the help of three friends and it was fully explored in 1908.   I sent several pieces of scoria to Workington for analysis that yielded 40 per cent. of iron, and some pieces that I sent from a mound at Far Owlers, Marsden, contained 53 per cent.   The ore at Cudworth and at other places was smelted in an open furnace by charcoal, and could be reduced only to a pasty mess and then hammered out into bars.   A piece of un-smelted ore was found in Cudworth and identified as hematite iron from the Barrow district.   In Elizabeth's time the charcoal furnace was suppressed in the High Furness district on account of the great destruction of timber, and from this suppression we may assume that in order to carry on their business, the smelters came to our moorland cloughs and brought the ore to the wood. The distance is roughly a hundred miles, and only packhorses could get to Cudworth and South Clough in Diggle. The now treeless Oaken Hill is near Cudworth, and when the name was first imposed it would be descriptive of the place, and its oaks would be cut down to make charcoal. The antiquary, Leland, writing of Blackley about 1550 says, "For lack of woode the blow shoppes (charcoal furnaces) decay there".

In 1907 I had the luck to unearth an actual furnace in Cudworth and I have since learned that it is an extremely rare find in the Pennines. I have not seen, read or heard of another, though I imagine that others have been found in the north hematite districts. It is believed that when the smelters had used up all the available timber in the clough they destroyed the furnaces. In 1760, the Rev. John Watson, saw an iron forge near Castleshaw, and called it "a piece of antiquity". It would no doubt be a mound of scoria from a charcoal furnace. It may be that the local smith brought the ore from High Furness, smelted it and made his own implements. If he did there is no local record of it. The furnace at Cudworth was destroyed by visitors, but not before it had been photographed. A full report appears in one of my books, and on the 23rd of July, 1898, I stood on a mound of iron slag at Cudworth and gave an account of my bloomery explorations to the members of the Lancashire and Cheshire Archaeological Society. After finding the furnace I grew weary of spade work and turned to local history and the making of verses. I published a few pieces of verse in a local newspaper and as usual, incurred the wrath of a few village pedagogues who had never looked with approval on anything that I had done. One of the poems, "The Watermill", was taken from the local paper and published in American magazines to shew the contrast between an old and a modern mill. I published my lines on Saddleworth Church in sheet form, and the Rev. Hugh Doig read them from the pulpit to an evening congregation. In the following week I received a letter from him in which he invited me to call at the vicarage. I replied accepting the invitation, but did not call. One day he came to Bankfield Mill to see me. They rung me up from the office and I went down to meet him. When I offered him my hand, he held back and said "I want to see Ammon Wrigley". "You are looking at him" I said, "I work here". I need hardly say how surprised he was, and after a chat I promised to go to the vicarage. After making several more promises and failing to keep them, I went to his house one Saturday night in midwinter. There was frozen snow on the ground and a fierce north east wind blowing from the moors, and as I had no overcoat I felt like a walking icicle when a maid opened the door. I found Mr. Doig in his study and after a little talk about the severity of the weather he said, "Let me see Mr. Wrigley, you are teetotal".

"Yes sir" I replied telling a lie that came out before I had time to think. He rang a bell and when a maid came into the room he said, "Bring this gentleman a bottle of cider, and bring me the usual".

The maid smiled as she left the room and I thought it was because she saw the gentleman was without collar or tie. I was wondering what the "usual" meant but I soon knew, for she came in with a bottle of cider for the gentleman, and a bottle of whisky, a jug of hot water and a basin of sugar for the parson. What a fool I had been for not telling the truth. It was the first time I had been in a parson's study, and I felt strangely awed for there seemed to be a solemnity and a kind of sacredness in the room more deep and impressive than any funeral service that I had ever heard. I thought it was the room in which Mr. Doig said his prayers, and if I had not seen it, I would not have believed that anything stronger than cider had been set on its table. In a flash the bottle of whisky and the smell of the spirit had rushed all the room's sacredness up the chimney. There I sat with a bottle of icy cold cider on a winter's night watching a man at my elbow dip his beak into hot whisky, and only by going through a similar experience can you feel how I felt. The reason why Mr. Doig had asked me to call and see him, was to hear how he could read my lines on Saddleworth Church, and I have often heard them read, but no one has ever approached Mr. Doig's reading in modulation and impressiveness. He let me out at the front door, and I beat even time in running to the Church Inn where I got cobblers of hot rum to bore a hole through the lump of frozen cider in my stomach. A large part of the Saddleworth Church poem was set to music by the late Mr. Albert Hudson, Mus. Bac. and it is still regarded as an exceptionally fine work. It was published and sung as the chief item at a concert given by the Saddleworth Vocal Society in the Mechanics Hall, Uppermill. I received a special invitation to be present, and on the Saturday night I left home with the intention of hearing it sung. When I reached Uppermill, I felt afraid of going into the Hall, and I went into the Globe Inn and stayed there till the concert was over. In some way copies of my "Friezland Ale" song got to America, and a poet wrote a song in praise of it. Here is the last verse :

> "Old England's Rose will e'er display,
> Its rarest fairest petal,
> As long as Saddleworth can say,
> That Friezland Ale's in fettle".

J. D. Law, Philadelphia.

Three of my friends, Mr. Arthur Radcliffe, Mr. Eli Smith, and Mr. Hugh Beech have set some of my poems to music and they are sung at Fellowship concerts.

I am a poor visitor, and under pressing invitations I have promised to visit many people and never gone near their houses. Some promises I have broken I have lived to regret, but none more than when I failed to visit a late Bishop of Lincoln. He wrote inviting me to stay with him at the Palace for a week or longer if I cared, so that he could show me the treasures of the Cathedral and the historic places in the city. I replied thanking him, and said that I worked in a mill and could not get away for a week. We were not strangers, for I knew him when he was Canon Hicks in Manchester, and I had been told that he was the head of the city's Temperance movement, and it was not the fear of having to drink pop and cider that kept me away from Lincoln. I had also been

THE LATE MR. THOMAS THOMPSON

told that he was one of the finest classical scholars in the north, and one hot summer's day I had been with him and Mr. Bruton on the Roman Camp at Castleshaw. On leaving we went round by the Horse and Jockey Inn, and I was gasping for a drink, but afraid to mention it before Canon Hicks. My thirst insisted, and I thought I'll risk it, so I said half pleadingly "may I have a drink here". "Yes, Ammon if you like, we'll wait for you" he said. And they did. I did not need twice telling, and I ran into the Jockey, and put two quick ones down. At his suggestion the lines I had written about Castleshaw appear in Appendix C, of Mr. Bruton's books on the Fort, and Professor Bosanquet of Liverpool University sent for 30 copies of the verse for the use of the students. I met many famous men during the explorations and one of the most interesting was Sir William Boyd Dawkins. One Saturday afternoon I spent a memorable hour with Mr. J. L. Paton, the Head Master of Manchester Grammar School. With trowels we were digging bits of grey ware out of the side of a trench.

THOMAS THOMPSON

A Mr. Thompson had come to live at Dale House, Delph, and I had been told that he wished to meet me, but I had no wish to meet him and I kept out of his way. I could not have given a sound reason for my attitude, but I simply did not want to see him. One lovely Sunday evening a gentleman came to my door at Hilltop and introduced himself as Mr. Thompson. I had just reached home after a day on the moors and my clothes were lavishly daubed with peat and clay. He wished to know if I would go with him to Moorside where he had two horses at a farm. I said that nothing would give me greater pleasure, and I took him a short cut through the fields beyond Shiloh. On our way back, he said "I understand you have many things that are worth publishing".

I said, "I have a lot of stuff parcelled up, but I have no opinion about it, and I am afraid it is of no value".

65

E

On the following evening he came again and I found him a parcel containing the manuscript of Saddleworth Superstitions, and he took it away to be published in Oldham. From that evening we saw much of each other, and he was so pleasant a companion that I had been a fool for refusing to meet him. We went roving over the moors and he caught the flint hunting fever. It was a change from the town life, and he seemed to have a boy's carefree joyousness in crossing cloughs and wading knee deep through bracken and moorgrass. March Hill and Warcock Hill are famous flint yielding sites, but they are on privately owned moors and Mr. Thompson did not wish to trespass on them, but after a time I overcame his objections and we had no trouble with gamekeepers. What happy carefree weekends we had out on the moors, and how we lingered and chatted over our teas of fried ham and eggs at old roadside inns. On going outside we sat on a form and lit our pipes for a restful smoke and watched the summer haze come like a dream over the evening moors. In 1912, he suggested that I should publish a book of prose and verse, and said if there were a loss he would pay it, but there was no loss, so he had nothing to pay.

The "Superstitions", now scarce, did not sell, and I did not wish to risk another failure. I got no help from local newsagents though I offered them threepence a copy out of a shilling booklet and it left nothing for myself. I took twelve copies to one shopman, and nine months later I called to see him and he reached them down from a high shelf. He had not sold a copy, and they had evidently been kept where no villager could see them. They were dust soiled, and I put them under my arm and went out of the shop using language anything but saintly. I did no better with other newsagents, and concluded that they intended to suppress me by not offering my booklets for sale. After thinking over Mr. Thompson's suggestion, I took my M.S. to publishers at Uppermill, and they gave me an estimate for 600 copies of an illustrated book. It was published by subscription, and I sent out a circular that brought me many orders and Mr. Thompson got a number from friends in Oldham. Locally the book caused a kind of mild sensation, and it was generally described as the most original and interesting work that had come from the pen of a Saddleworth born man. On April 2nd, 1913, gentlemen of the parish gave me a public dinner at the Globe Inn, Uppermill, and presented me with a cheque for 100 guineas and a timepiece for my wife. I thanked them in seven verses, and here are the first and last :

"There are times in our lives when words are weak,
Or at best come blindly groping their way,
When the heart is too moved by feeling to speak
From the tongue all that we would like to say.

Now, I say my last word, and my frail verse ends,
With a hope that wherever you may be,
As long as you live may you ever find friends
As jannock to you, as you are to me".

I reached home on that night with two bottles of whisky and two obstinate legs that had tried to go every way except the right one, but after a lot of coaxing they managed to drag me home where I received a defamatory lecture from the missus. At the close I moved a vote of thanks to the lecturer which was so badly received that I went to bed repentant but unforgiven.

About this time I got into trouble with chapel folks in the village. They told me that every Sunday morning Mr. Thompson had attended their chapel, and said, "He never comes now, and you have ruined him". "I have just done the opposite" I said, "he is pent up all the week in a town, and now he gets out on the hills every Sunday, with the wind blowing the dust out of his lungs, and feels much better than sitting in a musty pew with a collection box under his nose". For a time I did little writing, but at last the fit came upon me again and in 1916 I published "The Wind Among the Heather", and it was just out, when a deep and lasting sorrow fell upon my life. Mr. Thompson died of cancer and I lost the best friend, the sincerest wellwisher, and the most generous helpmate that I have ever known. Kindness and helpfulness formed the bedrock of his nature, and without his ceaseless encouragement I should not have published any work of mine in book form. I had found that publishing booklets was a losing game, and it was my intention to go on writing prose sketches and verse to newspapers.

THE SNUFF TAKER

One cold Saturday when I had been seeking flints on Cupwith Moor, I went along the road to the important Roman Station at Slacks Farm, Outlane. I had been told that the Roman tiles built in the field walls were imperishable, and on seeing them I felt inclined to believe it. On my way home I called at a roadside inn and sat down in the taproom by the side of a big hefty Yorkshireman. He had a strong weather tanned face and appeared to be about fifty years of age. He was without coat, his waistcoat loose from top to bottom, and his shirt open showing a chest as brown as leather. I noticed that his pot was empty and I said, "Will you have a drink with me". "Yus, aw will lad, bring a pint Joe, an' keep thi thumb aht". When he had been served, he took a snuff box out of his waistcoat pocket and said, "just try a pinch o' this". "What brand is it"? I asked. "Top Mill" he replied, "nah its reight snuff, gooid for th' yedwark". I am no snuff taker but I took a pinch for friendliness, and when I had done sneezing, I said, "You appear to work out of doors". "Yus" he said, "aw work op o' th' rooads an' mi shirt neck hasn't been buttoned this last twenty year, winter nor summer". "What do you live on" I asked, "that keeps you hale and hearty, and able to stand rough weather on this high bleak road". "Aw get plenty o' rooast beef, an' aw loike shuet dumplins, but aw want shuet cut i' big lumps soa as it sticks aht o' th' sides o' th' dumplins loike cat een".

He then took a snuff box out of his other waistcoat pocket, and said "Try a pinch o' this, it smells loike Yorkshire rooases". "What is it" I said. "Tom Buck" he replied, "It'll mak thi jump ovver th' sun". I took a pinch and said "Why do you take two kinds of snuff". "Nah does tha see" he replied,

"Aw Top Mill for one nose hoil, an' Tom Buck for th' tother nose hoil, aw nivver let one o' mi nose hoils join at two boxes". "I know men and women who take snuff, and one man who takes it with a teaspoon when he is at home, but you are the first man that I have met who carries two brands of snuff in his pockets". He was worth staying with, but I had to leave and get over the moorlands before nightfall. I left him the price of a pint, and set out for Buckstones.

Cambodunum, is the Roman name for the camp at Outlane, and a hypocaust found during the excavations in 1865 is now set up in the grounds of the Tolson Memorial Hall, Huddersfield.

MATT SANDFORD

I well remember my first meeting with Matt the famous caricaturist. He was then living in Manchester, and working for the Daily Dispatch and other papers. One fine Saturday evening two Oldham gentlemen came to my house, and one of them said, "Will you go up to Greenfield for an hour, just for a change"?

"I don't mind" I said, "I am at a loose end", but had I known what was in the wind and that it had been arranged for a given purpose, I would not have gone a yard. On leaving Greenfield station, we sauntered on to the Clarence Inn. There were six or seven gentlemen in the best room including one that I had not seen before—the others I knew intimately. As we sat talking I noticed that the stranger appeared to be making sketches of me in a book he had on his knees. He said something to Jim Redford, and they came across the room to where I sat, and Jim said, "This is Matt of the Daily Dispatch and he would like you to go with him into another room, do you mind". "Not at all" I said, and we went into an empty room where he made about four sketches of me, and I learned that he had to paint my portrait in watercolour. On the following Saturday evening he brought the finished painting to the Clarence Inn, for a room half full of gentlemen to say what they thought about it. Some of them said it was a good portrait, but I thought the opposite and said nothing. Other gentlemen said the nose was wrong. Matt had put a big plum coloured nose on my face, that people might see how beautifully I made it with drinking Friezland Ale. I was painted standing by a table with a pot full of ale near my right hand. It was decided that the portrait should be framed in Manchester and presented to me at a public dinner to be held at the Clarence Inn. Just before we broke up, I asked if I might take the picture home to show my wife and family. They said yes, but I must see that it went to Manchester, and a gentleman could call for it at my house. I took it home and the moment I entered the house it went on the fire. There was a bit of trouble about my destroying it and Matt wanted me to sit again, but I refused. I learned afterwards that Jim Redford had suggested the plum coloured nose, and the pot of ale, and I said the painting might be suitable for a taproom, but not for a house room. I met Matt several times when he came to visit Jim Redford, and we had friendly drinks together.

His best work is said to have been done in the press gallery of the House of Commons, after he went to live in London. I believe Lady Astor took the pencil from him and said, "you have got my hat wrong".

AN OIL PAINTING

One sunny afternoon a gentleman came to my door and when I opened it he said "Are you Mr. Ammon Wrigley".

"I believe I am" I replied.

"Can I take your photograph".

I then noticed that he had a camera and I said, "I have been so much photographed and written about by newspaper men, that now I am rather afraid of them".

"I am not a newspaper man" he said, "I come from London, and staying with relations at Hyde, I heard of you".

As he had come so far I thought it would be churlish of me to refuse, so leading the way into the garden I said, "Come along and I will pose for you".

He took three photographs and I thought so little about it, that I allowed him to leave without getting his name and address. When months had passed I heard that an oil painting of me was on exhibition at Stockport. I was mystified, and could not imagine who had painted it or how it had come to be exhibited. Thinking I might get to know something about it, I went to Stockport and the moment I saw the picture I knew that it had been painted by the gentleman who had taken the photograph in our garden. Two men were looking at it, and one with a catalogue said, "It's Ammon Wrigley of Saddleworth, and I've heard the Corporation are going to buy it". As usual I had a cap on my head, a white cotton scarf round my neck, and was wearing the old grey suit in which I had been photographed and is seen in the picture. I thought the men might notice that I was like the picture and I went and stood in a corner of the room with my back towards them. When they had gone out I went and had a good look at it, and decided to try and get in touch with the artist. When I had got his name and address I wrote to him and eventually bought the picture, and it is now the property of The Oldham Corporation and is hung in the Art Gallery. It was painted by Harry Rutherford, an artist of repute, who has exhibited at the Royal Academy exhibitions for many years.

SIR SAMUEL BRIGHOUSE

Sir Samuel Brighouse was one of the most interesting men that I have ever met. He had read my books and wished to meet me, but when he came to Oldham I failed to turn up. It was then arranged that I should meet him and other gentlemen at the Moorcock Inn, a lively place on Waddington Fell. I knew that he had been a Lancashire coroner for nearly half a century, and going along in my friend's car I wondered if the holding of many inquests had given him a gloomy outlook on life. On

71

reaching the Moorcock I soon found that he was a jovial hail-fellow man who would be loved in any company. He had done much holiday tramping in out of way country places, met many quaint old characters and swiped pints of ale in roadside inns with ploughmen and roadmenders, and how racily he could describe his jaunts and uncommon experiences. For me it had been a memorable day and in the evening when we were about to leave he said "Ammon I want you to do me a favour".

"What kind of favour" I asked surprised.

"I am 86 years of age" he said "and this is my doctor. Now I want you to promise that if he does not keep me alive till I am 90, you will shoot the devil".

Of course I promised, and when he was 90 years I sent him some congratulatory verse and asked for leave to sell my gun. "Yes" he replied, "the doctor has kept me alive because I had told him that you were a dead shot". Perhaps with fairplay I could hit a hay stack at twenty yards range. The last time I met him was at the Masonic Temple in Manchester, and during lunch he began to tell his tales in a way that always seemed to me inimitable. One tale he told, I often recall when I see children going to school. I had said something about school children, and Sir Samuel said, "When I go down the street in a morning for my paper, the children who pass me say ever so nicely, Good morning, Sir Samuel, and I say, Good morning children, but when you go down the other side of the street you say, owd Sammy's going down again". "Oh no, we do not say that, Sir Samuel". The way in which he told that simple tale was most amusing and for me unforgetable.

SAM FITTON

I had known Sam Fitton for years and when he came to live in Oldham we became boon companions. He came to my house like coming home, and on fine evenings we wandered among the heather on Highmoor, and what merry hours we spent in homely country inns, and what songs we sang at night down the hilly road to the famous old inn at Austerlands. We loved it, and I could tramp the length and breadth of Yorkshire and not find a homelier or better conducted inn than the Royal Tiger in Miss Turner's day. She was an elderly spinster and had been born in the house, and in a way she ruled the conversation among the customers. I heard her stop strangers who had called and begun to talk about betting and horse racing. Swearing was not permitted, and she would have no loose talk about religion, and particularly against the Church of England. The living room was the public room and so scrupulously clean that you could have eaten your dinner from the flagstones of the floor. When they had been scrubbed on a Saturday morning she covered them with old newspapers for our dirty feet to walk over. The room was rich in old fashioned furnishings, an old oak panelled langsettle with a long print cushion, grandfathers clock with a moon dial, corner cupboard and spindle backed rush-seated chairs, and everything in it seemed to be dreaming of bygone days. It was the clock that inspired Sam Fitton to write one of his most famous poems "My old Case Clock". When Miss Turner died, the house lost its character, and rank tangled grass now grows where Sam sung and recited on many a memorable night. He was amazingly versatile, a playwright, actor, artist, mimic, singer and an inimitable entertainer. As a dialect writer he ranks with the finest Lancashire has ever known. He died in 1923 and in 1929 I published as I had promised him "Gradely Lancashire"; a book of his prose and verse and if there is another book in the Lancashire dialect that is more packed with humour I do not know of it. For years he contributed a weekly article to an Ashton paper, and occasionally illustrated it with thumbnail sketches. He had asked the Factory Times people to publish his book, but they refused. In 1911 he began to publish The Crompton Chanticleer, a humourous monthly that for want of support came to an end with about seven numbers. He is buried in Crompton Cemetery. That there is no fitting public memorial to him makes one think that Shaw people have either forgotten or do not appreciate the work of a man who has placed their townlet on the literary map of Lancashire. Surely there must be a few who remember the man that wrote the racy "Unofficial Guide to Shay", "Eaur Market Neet" and other poems relating to the district. Sam Fitton will live in the hearts of all lovers of the Lancashire dialect, and as long as the dialect lasts. I have omitted to say that he was a member of the Lancashire Authors Association, and the chief and most original of its laughter makers.

THE SPECTRE OF THE BROCKEN

One Whit-Sunday noon about 1925 I called at the Floating Light Inn, a house that stands high up on the windy edge of Stanedge moors. It was then a homely old inn, dear to the moorend folks and to many wayfarers like myself. It was built in 1840 by Johnny Wrigley, a famous Stanedger in his day, and at one time three lifeboys were painted on its signboard, but its licence is now held by an imposing newly built swagger inn. I had just been served with a glass of ale when two strangers came into the room, and the moment they spoke to each other their dialect told me that they had come from the Huddersfield district. They ordered two glasses of ale and when the waiter had set them on the table one man turned to the other and said, "Aw nivver teld thi abaat yer Joa seein' a gret giant on th' rooad at th' Isle o' th' Skye woakin abaat i' th' mist, tother Sunday".

"It would be the Spectre of the Brocken" I broke in, curious to know more about it.

"Nah aw dont know abaat that" he said, "But yer Joa wer flayed aht o' his wits an' he ran into th' aleheause an' teld a chap, an' thi went aht but th' giant had gone some rooad".

"I heard of a shepherd" I said, "who saw the Spectre on Rishworth moor, and he went home for the day as he thought it meant bad luck to go among his sheep, but I will give you my experience. One Sunday morning in the summer of 1908 I saw

74

the Spectre on Friarmere moor, and it is referred to in a Saddleworth book published in 1909. There was sunshine and mist, and I had just reached the moortop when the huge figure of a man appeared in the mist about twenty or thirty yards away and in front of me".

"Yar Joa said his giant wor in a mist, wat did yors do" ?

"It did nothing" I replied, "but I was terrified and about to run off the moor, when the figure began to fade, and I then knew it was the Spectre of the Brocken that I had read is sometimes seen in the Highlands of Scotland. It was my own shadow, greatly magnified and thrown upright on the mist by the sun, instead of along the ground. A gamekeeper told me that the Quiet Shepherd Inn, (now closed) on Longdendale hills, was so named from an old shepherd who had spoken to the Spectre on Kinder Scout Moor, but getting no word from it, he called his inn, The Quiet Shepherd".

"Haa is it it's coaled Spectre of the Brocken?" one of the men asked.

"I used to wonder why" I replied, "but one day I read in a book that the name came from the Brocken, one of the highest summits of the Hartz Mountains in Germany, where magnified shadows are frequently seen in sunshine and mist".

"Awst tell yar Joa wat yo've teld us".

"I believe the Spectre is rarely seen among the Pennines" I said, "and in all my roaming of the moors I have seen it once only. I do not know whether other people have seen it in Saddleworth. Well I'm off now on to Warcock Hill".

"Nah cahr thi dahn, an' get a drink wi us".

"No thanks, not this morning, I am late as it is. I have a friend to meet".

STONE TENTER POSTS.

In a field near Wallhill, Saddleworth, there is what I believe to be one of the most remarkable outdoor relics of bygone textile industrialism to be found in Lancashire, or in the West Riding of Yorkshire. It is a row of stone tenter posts, and seen from the main Huddersfield road they make an imposing sight on the hillside. I had seen no reference to them in local records, or learned anything about them from people living in the district, but on an old map I found that they were described as tenters. On going to see them it appeared to be the right description. I then wrote to a friend of mine, Mr. W. B. Crump of Leeds, the author of The History of the Woollen Industry, in the Huddersfield district, including Saddleworth. With my letter I sent him a photograph of the stones, and in his reply he said they formed a most unusual and interesting relic of bygone industrialism. He had never seen, heard or read of anything like them. Originally the row was unbroken, but it is now divided by a field wall. Parts of each stone have been cut away in order to fix the wooden frames that held the hooks to which the pieces were attached, and the bolt holes may still be seen. The Highmoor quarries are near, and the maker of the cotton or flannel pieces may have owned or had interest in one of the quarries.

I sent a photograph of them to Mr. C. Stott, the Chief Lbrarian of Rochdale, and he wrote for the film, and now a large framed photograph of the Wallhill Tenter Stones, is in the Council room or at the Free Library.

There are 15 stones and they stand about 8 feet apart. They are nearly six feet high, 16 inches wide at the side, and 7 inches at the front and are estimated to weigh one ton each.

THE WOOLWALL AT DELPH.

A remarkably fine example of the old woolwall may be seen across the field in front of Lower Hilltop House, on the road from Delph to Grains Bar. It is five feet wide at the base, and tapering to one foot at the top. On the side facing the road it is built up of many small stones in the form of steps on which the dyed or scoured wool was spread to be dried in the sun. It was built solely for drying wool, and is the only woolwall I have seen or ever heard of either in Saddleworth or elsewhere. I have not measured it, but I think it is thirty yards long. There is a small dam near the house that supplied the water for dyeing or scouring.

"DOG HUNTING"

My favourite moor sport is what moormen call "dog hunting", from the middle of July to the early days of August, when young birds are well on the wing. It is an innocent sport, there is no "fluttering gory pinion", as Burns sings, and I think one of the most interesting and enjoyable sights on a moor is to watch two or three well trained dogs back each other up at a "set". How quietly and gently they raise one foot and then another as they approach the bird or birds. They might be stepping on air and if the men behind them make the least noise, the dogs look round in a way that means silence you fools. What good protective colouring a moor affords to grouse. One Saturday afternoon about the end of July I went with three gentlemen and three dogs on to Friarmere moor, and as we were leaving Hind hill, the leading dog made a "set" and the other dogs caught the scent, and in a minute a small table cloth would have covered them. The first dog was looking at something in the grass about a yard from its nose. We all four looked and better looked as they say, but could see nothing, and at last one of the gentlemen said "It is a bird that has just gone and left a strong scent behind it". With that we went forward, but the dogs would not follow, and we had to go back to them. We had been looking for some time and seen nothing, when a gentleman said, "I see the bird", and he picked up a plump hen grouse from under a dog's nose. With the dog so near it the bird must have been incapable of flight, for when tossed up it was soon away over Clowes moor.

One Sunday evening coming over Hellpit Edge moor my dog "set" at something near the path. I looked but could see nothing, and went on but the dog would not come to my whistle, and I went back and groping among the grass I put my hand on a full grown lapwing. When thrown up it flew strongly across the valley towards a house that I had been told was called "Pins i' th' Bacon" because a man who had lived there stuck pins in the bacon so that his wife could not eat any when he was out.

DATED STONES ON OLD BUILDINGS

For years I corresponded with the late Mr. Richard Heape of Healey Hall, Rochdale, and when he was collecting data for his monumental work "Inscribed and Dated Stones and Sundials in and adjoining the Ancient Parish of Rochdale", I furnished him with many dated stones from old Saddleworth houses. In his Introduction he refers to the help I had given him, but unfortunately I am described as the "Saddleworth Historian" ; a description that I feel cannot be applied to me. In one of his letters he said "I am ill and I intend to give my manuscript to the Rochdale Free Library". He wrote a very minute hand, and in my reply I said that there would be great difficulty in reading his manuscript and I hoped that he would soon be well and publish it in book form. His health improved and he published it without letting me know, and I had collected thirty dates from old Saddleworth buildings that are not in his book, including one from Castleshaw dated 1642, the first year of the Rebellion. It was published by the University Press, Cambridge, a limited issue at four guineas each. When the book was out, he wrote and asked me if there was a public library in Saddleworth where a copy would be cared for and treasured. I replied that I did not know of one, and suggested that he should send a copy to the Oldham Lyceum or The Free Library. Just before his death he sent me a print of a painting of himself on horseback as Master of the

Rochdale Hunt, with the hounds round him and Healey Hall in the background.

Note—In 1708 and for years afterwards the Heape family were farmers at Grange in the Castleshaw valley.

ALPHABET STONES

I never knew a dame school, but I knew a man with the nickname of Ned o'th Schoo Dames, so his mother must have kept a dame school. From old men who had attended dame schools in their young days I got all that appears in my books about them. One can believe that they were unruly places, for an elderly woman with a school in her cottage living room would have something to do to keep order among noisy and mischievous youngsters. In front of the Mermaid Inn at Hollingworth near the Lake of that name, I saw a flagstone with the capital letters of the alphabet carved on it. I had heard about such stones but it was the first I had seen. On going into the inn I found that the living room was the public room with old fashioned furnishings. The landlady an elderly woman, was on her knees before the fire kneading dough in a big mug, and I had to wait till she had finished before I got served with a glass of ale. She told me that on summer evenings the hamlet fathers sat outside with their pots of ale and made the children say the alphabet from the stone. The next time I visited Hollingworth, the inn was closed and the alphabet stone had disappeared. I looked round but failed to find it. I then asked a friend, Mr. Harry Percival of Smithy Bridge, to look for it, and he found two alphabet stones, one with capital and the other with small letters carved on the interior flagstones of an occupied cottage. I then wrote to Mr. C. Stott, the curator of the Rochdale Museum, and told him they were relics of the dame school age, and should be in the Museum or in one of the town's public schools. He and Mr. Percival went to the cottage and got the address of the owner, and on approaching him he refused to part with the stones, and the letters will probably get worse for wear.

BUTT SHOOTING

I have never taken part in a grouse drive ; it was not a sport to my liking, but I have seen birds shot at the butts and I know that some people condemn it as butchery. They are generally people who have never seen it, yet they appear to think that grouse are driven almost down the gun barrel. They are wrong, for when I have seen seven or eight grouse coming towards a butt the man with the gun has always marked at an outside bird. Had he sent the shot wildly into the pack he would probably have wounded three or four birds that could not be gathered. They would have flown away with pellets in them and pined to death on the moors. That kind of shooting would soon thin a moor of its grouse. I have heard shooters say that a bird coming fast towards the gun is more difficult to kill than one that is going away from it. Of course the nearer the gun and the more concentrated the shot. A gentleman who was one of the best shots in Yorkshire from the trap, came with a party to shoot over a moor that was under a gamekeeper friend of mine. He said "how I cursed when I knew that chap was coming for I thought he'll play havoc with my birds, but at the first drive he had not a bird down because they were coming towards him. Had they been going away from him, he would have killed them.

A LANCASHIRE NEET

At the request of a friend who was in India I wrote a few dialect verses descriptive of a Lancashire night concert that was to be held at the Lyceum, Oldham. They were to be recited as the opening item of the programme. When I entered the Lyceum on that night I found the assembly room packed with ladies and gentlemen who were probably members, and I had a difficulty in finding a back seat.

When my lines had been recited a gentleman came to the front of the platform and said "There are three Lancashire writers in the room, will you please stand up so that people may

80

WOOLWALL AT DELPH

see them ? I was surprised when Sam Fitton and Joe Cronshaw got up from one of the front seats. They had been sat together and turning to Sam, Cronshaw said, "an' does theau seh 'at awm feawer nur thee".

It was loud enough for everyone in the room to hear, and Sam replied, "Ay, aw wouldn't ha come here to neet if mi face wur as feaw as thine".

"Theau'd look a bit better if theau'd wipe thi nose", Joe said and in that way they went on for ten minutes amid continuous laughter. I had not stood up and a man on my right said "Get up Ammon, you are "feawer" than both of them. Now is your chance, you'll win easily". To stand up with nothing to say seemed a ridiculous thing to do, and I remained seated.

AT THE BOOKSHOPS

One day I went into a second-hand bookshop in Manchester, and as I stood looking round the well-packed shelves a smartly dressed shopman came up to me and said, "Are you looking for some particular book" ?

"Yes", I said, "The Wind Among the Heather, have you a copy" ?

"We have, but I think it is above your price" he replied.

He had evidently noticed that I was without a collar and that my worn trousers were very baggy at the knees.

"What are you prepared to pay for it" ? he asked.
"About six shillings if it is in good condition" I replied.
He laughed, and said, "I want two pounds for it".

"You will want a long time before you get two pounds out of me, it is not worth it" I said.

"Anything else you want" ?
"No, not to-day".

F

On going out into the street I wondered what he would have said if I had told him that I was the author of the book. He might have 'phoned the police station and said, "There's a man in my shop who is not fit to be at large, he claims to be an author, come and look at him".

At Huddersfield, a second-hand bookseller had two copies of "Wind Among the Heather" and I thought this man does not know what they are asking for the book in Manchester, and I'll take the two copies if the price is reasonable. I took one out of the shelves and said "What do you want for this".

"Thirty-five shillings" he replied.

"You're joking" I said, "I'll give you five shillings for it".

"Thirty-five, not a penny less" he said emphatically, "It's by a Saddleworth man, and was published in Huddersfield".

"I suppose he would get about five shillings for it, and you're asking thirty-five".

"Take it or leave it" he said.

"I shall leave it, good morning".

One night at a Waterhead inn, a friend said "I've seen one of your books "The Wind Among the Heather" in a shop window marked 7s. 6d. I drank up and caught the first car to Cross Street. As soon as I entered the shop I laid three halfcrowns on the counter. "What is that for" the shopman asked, "It's for "The Wind Among the Heather" " I said. "Yes, but it is thirty-seven and six pence" he said, "It is one of the scarcest books in Lancashire and this is the first copy I have ever seen".

I went to Waterhead and said some rude things to my friend. He said "I must have missed the figure three,—get a bottle of Bass".

I had similar experiences when trying to buy copies of my other books.

BAKING

In my young days every village and daleswoman baked her own bread. There were no bread vans rushing about the roads with loaves as black as the devil's nutting poke, and crusts like leather. Home baked bread is still the sweetest and most wholesome that can be put into the mouth. When my mother had kneaded her dough she made the sign of the cross on it to make it rise well. Some women used milk instead of water when kneading and it was said to make the best bread. Very little confectionery was made in the village, a bit of parkin and robin cake, and a few crumpets. Home baked oatcake once so common, had ceased to be made in my day. It had passed into business and a man with a horse and trap used to hawk it round the district. We had about six leaves hung on our breadfleck every week, and it could be seen in inn kitchens, but it is now a thing of the past. Snuff taking was very common, and some women were said to take it when kneading their dough, and an old bachelor was said to take snuff till his loaves looked like brown bread. When yeast in a solid form first came into our village it was called "papper birm", because it was wrapped in paper.

COTTAGE FURNISHINGS

Furniture was much alike in the dale and village homes. Our furniture at Millcroft may be taken as typical of what could be seen in most houses. We had an old oak chest, corner cupboard, langsettle with a panelled back, a deal table and five or six rush bottomed chairs. A man called Scatteram, used to come round the district with a big sheaf of rushes on his back for mending chairs. Carpets were scarce in the hillside houses, and every Saturday the house floor was sprinkled with fresh crushed sand and the hearthstone decorated with curious designs done in blue "idleback", a chalk like substance that was hawked round the hamlets by a man with a little donkey and cart. I used to go to him for two pennyworth of "idleback" and never thought that the strange word meant laziness, and I do not know how it got that name.

INN CUSTOMS

The old customs common to some village and countryside inns died out before the war of 1914, and have not known a revival and probably never will. At Christmas, warm mulled ale and currant bread were set before the customers. At Shrovetide a big mug of batter was set on the taproom table and a string stretched high up across the room, and every man who made a pancake was expected to throw it over the string and catch it in the pan as it came down. At Wakes time free ale was served to casual callers and customers. Every night at some inns the landlords handed cigars out to the company in the best room. There were match stands on the taproom tables that held a box of matches for the use of smokers, and in winter a pot of freshly mixed mustard and a spoon were set on the table so that men could put a spoonful in their ale to give it a kick and keep them free from rheumatism. I think taproom manners are better to-day. Two friends would join at pints of ale and pay in their turn and drink in turn out of the same pot. I used to think it was a dirty habit, especially if they were smoking or chewing twist tobacco.

AN INN SIGN

One Sunday night I called at the old Hanging Gate Inn, Weakey, where Elliot Sykes was the landlord. We had been good friends for years, and I always looked in when I chanced to be in Diggle. It was rather early, about half past seven, and I did not expect to find many people in the house. It happened that I was the first customer and I found Elliot sitting alone by the fire in the best room. "It's a black night" I said, "There isn't a star to be seen. I had meant to climb over Harrop Edge, but I might loose the path".

"Yes" he said, "It's best to keep to the main road, it's a rough track over Harrop Edge".

When I had been served with a drink we sat smoking and staring at the fire, for Elliot seemed in the dumps and in no mood for talking. Thinking I would stir him I said, "You are slack to-night".

84

"Yes" he said, "It's early, they'll be showing up afore long".

In the silence that followed I fell to thinking about the rhyme on the gate over the inn door, and remembered that the same rhyme was painted on the signboard of the Gate Inn, at the foot of Blackstone Edge moors. At last I said, "I can fill this house every night in the week". He said nothing and I concluded that he was not interested. I was mistaken for after another silence, he said, "Aw connut tell heaw theau'd fill this heause, aw connut do it".

"Why" I said, "It's the easiest matter in the world".

"Aw'd like to know heaw" he said.

"Well" I said, "What is the rhyme on the gate over your door"?

He recited it.

> "This gate hangs well and hinders none,
> Refresh and pay and travel on".

"To fill the house" I said, "All that you have got to do is to alter the rhyme and make it read,

> "This gate hangs well and hinders none,
> Come in and drink and set it on."

Of course "Set it on" meant get a skinful and pay nothing. He looked at me for a minute and then he eased himself with a fluent discharge of rich classical Weakey language that made me think of what "Diggle Joe" had given me one night at the Diggle Hotel. Finally Elliot said, "Theau goes sillier every time aw see thee". He never forgot it, and the last time I saw him, it was at the Commercial Inn, Uppermill, and the moment I entered the room he laughed and said, "Come in an' drink an' set it on".

85

GERMANS AT STANEDGE AND ISLE OF SKYE

I cannot fix the year, but I think it would be about 1912. One Saturday I saw a print of Marsden moors in the Illustrated London News, and it stated that they had been acquired by the Government as sites for what we now call aerodromes. I spent the next day Sunday on the moors and in the evening I called at the Great Western Inn, Stanedge. I was alone in the parlour looking at some pieces of flint that I had found on March Hill, when about twenty young Germans with cameras came into the room. When they had been served with beer they began to talk, some in German and others in English. One who sat near me said, "Do you live near this inn"? "No" I replied, "I live miles away. Where do you live"?

"Manchester" he replied.

I learned that they had been on Marsden moors taking photographs to send to their homes in Germany and I then knew that they had seen the print in the London News. They stayed about fifteen minutes and then one of them said something in German and they all hurried out of the room and up the road probably to go to Diggle Station.

I told a gentleman about it. He had been round the world two or three times and he said that in a straight line there was no higher ground between Marsden moors and the Carpathian Mountains. I said it seemed unbelieveable, and I do not know to this day whether he was right or wrong.

Not long afterwards an old friend of mine, the late Dr. T. W. Woodhead, at that time the principal of the Huddersfield Technical College, invited me by letter to meet him and some German Professors at Isle of Skye. He had told them in some correspondence that dead trees could be seen underlying the peat on the moors near Huddersfield. They doubted it and replied that they would come and see them. They came from Bonn University to Huddersfield, and were taken to Isle of Skye, but

86

it rained all day and I remained at the mill. Dr. Woodhead told me the Professors seemed more interested in seeing the country than looking at the dead trees. The best evidence of trees underlying the peat is on the Warcock Hill side of the Western Reservoir.

A SPINNING JENNY

A literary friend of mine, the late Mr. H. Ling Roth of Halifax, wanted to know if I could get him a little cottage spinning jenny for the industrial section of Bankfield Museum. He had failed to find one in the districts near his own town. I went to a mooredge farm where the people had given up manufacturing. They had a little jenny and wanted six pounds for it. I wrote Mr. Roth and told him it was in fairly good condition and he sent me a Corporation cheque for that amount. On the following Saturday he came over to Saddleworth and we went to the farm. "I have come to pay for the jenny" I said offering the cheque to one of the brothers, but the sister took it out of my hand. When she had looked at it for a few minutes she handed it to a brother and said "Dosto think it's a good un Bill"? Bill looked it over and shaking his head doubtfully said "It looks a queer un". When the other brother had seen it, all three went up the stairs taking the cheque with them. It amused Mr. Roth and he said, "They must think Halifax Corporation is not worth six pounds".

They were upstairs some time and when they came down the sister had the cheque in her hand and she said, "We think it's a good un but we'd o rayther had it i' gowd". Bill got a piece of paper to make out a receipt. It was in April and the sister spelt it letter by letter A-p-r-i-l. Mr. Roth bought other hand machines that would probably have been broken up for firewood. As we went up the lane he said, "There are still some interesting old characters on the Saddleworth mooredges. The people we have just left are I feel sure as honest and as straightforward as any you could meet in Yorkshire". "Yes I know they are" I said, "It is written on their faces. There is a character lives in the house over that field. During a coal strike he carried a sackful of coal on his back from the station in the valley. It was in winter and the weight of the coal made him sweat, so when he felt cold he got the sackful of coal on his back and carried it round the house till he became warm. He did not light his fire, he cooked his foodstuffs on a little paraffin stove".

I had the workroom at Deanhead photographed and it shows the little fifty spindled jenny, the bobbinwheel, part of the looms and the warping walls, skips, etc. I believe it is the only picture of a homestead workroom in the Huddersfield district.

THE FELLOWSHIP

The Fellowship was founded on August 27th, 1931, at an old homely tavern in Austerlands village, and when I saw a report of the first meeting in a local newspaper I decided to have nothing to do with it. The founders were personal friends of mine, and when I had been led to believe that it would be confined to them I withdrew my opposition. They broke their promises and by the end of 1932 the membership had grown to hundreds, and on January 21st, 1933, the first of the annual festivals took place in Oldham, and drew members of Parliament, mayors of boroughs, and other people. The publicity I received made me miserable and I failed to attend, which gave the local newspapers much copy. It is said to be the only Fellowship in England to a living scribbler. The membership is still growing and in the summer months there are rambles in the country and concerts in the evening. In winter meetings are held in Oldham, Rochdale, Rawtenstall, and other places.

I believe some members have never forgiven me for not making gramophone records so that my not too beautiful voice could be heard at the meetings. It has been stated in newspapers and at lectures that I refused Mr. Rudyard Kipling's request to make the records. I did not; it was what I had to go through after making them, that kept me out of London. Mr. Anthony Crossley and Mr. Kipling made all the arrangements with the Gramophone company, and when my recording was over I had to go to The House of Commons and have tea on the Terrace with four members of Parliament. Then I had to see the sights of London and finally go with Mr. Crossley to his house at Chelsea and stay there till his wife, an artist, had painted my portrait, and it was all that fuss that led me to stay in Oldham. I could not complain about the pay as it was good. Mr. Rudyard Kipling had promised Mr. Crossley that he would attend an annual meeting of the Fellowship in Oldham, but unfortunately he died before one came round. Mr. Crossley always said we were two vagabonds, and his last book "From one Vagabond to Another" is dedicated to me. By his untimely death I lost a very dear friend, and the Fellowship one of the best loved of its members. Here are some verses from the dedication poem.

To Ammon.

"The Curtain of autumnal mist shuts out the shaggy hill,
The lambs that leapt in April are yonder huddling sheep,
Through the cloughs, along the shaws, the wind rises
   and falls,
And the chinks of the grey walls whistle and the moisture
   mottles the stone.

The desire of the desolate hills tugs at your heart
The track pierces the heather familiar before you,
Ammon, the track is yours
To the cairn, the weathered symbol of the silence of the
   moors.

Linger not long in talk to-day, though you together share
The sum of the moorland wisdom from Pendle to the Peak
A song is loud in your head to the desolate refrain of the
   wind,
And ever the peat-path vanishes round yet another hill
   beyond.
Old solitary vagabond ! By grass and hag and heather, fare
Forward : Still, in the seeking, find all you seek,
Until all the last salient spur, you see beneath you through
   the blind,
Devouring dusk, with myriad lights the great towns
   grope at the hills.

89

Descend to the old stone hostel, the genial folk, the
generous ale,
The rain spurting on the windows, the merry song and
the moorland tale,
The peat high-piled upon the logs to hiss and crackle to
the gale."

From a review by William Beck, "It is one of the most
perfect of the poems in unity of impression and expression", and
of my work he says "He is a writer of clear sinewy and picturesque
prose both in dialect and standard English. He sets down the
graphic and essential word, and brightens the memory's treasure
trove and fruits of delving in old records with the insight of a poet".

I have regretted that I did not go to London and make
the gramophone records, but I felt afraid of the fine folks I had to
meet.

AN EDITOR IN 1910

It is often said that if an article is published in a newspaper it should be worth paying for, but editors keep their pockets
stitched with wire to beginners. I had articles and racy sketches
about country folks and countrysides published in various newspapers but it was not till 1910 that I received my first payment.
In that year Chapman and Hall, London, published a rather
imposing and well produced Monthly entitled "The Thrush".
It was devoted to poetry and criticism, and a friend suggested that
I should send the editor some of my verse, but when I saw a copy
containing poems by Norman Gale, John Drinkwater, Alfred
Noyes and other well established poets I felt that my stuff would
have little chance of acceptance. However, I sent "On a Yorkshire
Moor" a poem of 72 lines and it came back almost before I thought
it had reached London. I was about to throw the long envelope
in the fire when a letter dropped out and the editor said that if
I would alter four lines that he had indicated he would send me
a guinea. I could not see anything wrong with the lines, but
I altered them, and the guinea came along. To celebrate the

first money I had received from an editor, I "blued" some of it on mulled ale with friends at the Swan Inn in the village. Three poems from that month's "Thrush" were reviewed in the "Review of Reviews" published by W. T. Stead, and the reviewer said of my verse, "This poem breathes the very breath and ecstacy of the moors". Two verses were given, and thus encouraged I sent the editor, Walter Jerrold, another poem, and he returned it with a reply that owing to loss "The Thrush" had ceased publication.

After a day's roaming over the moors I always felt the urge to write rhymes, and part of the "West Wind in Spring" was written in the taproom at the Great Western Inn, Stanedge, and part of "The Green Road" at the Ram's Head Inn, Denshaw, and verses of "On a Yorkshire Moor" at Bill's o' Jack's, the name of an old moorland inn, not a person. In all my roaming I have not done what they say a Yorkshire man did one Easter Sunday on Wessenden moors. When he reached home at night his wife said "Where's that white napkin thi sandwich wur lapped in"?

"Wur it lapped in a napkin" he said feeling in his pockets.

"Igh theau knows it wur" she said, "It's weshin day i' morning".

"Well then" he said, "by gum lass, aw mun ha hettin it wi mi sandwich, an' nivver noticed it, but aw wur reight hungry".

We all have our likes and dislikes. I dislike fine functions and in my time I have ignored many invitations to them. I would rather hear an old moorman sing a home made country folk song in an inn corner than listen to an opera singer. I would rather eat bread and cheese at a taproom table with a shepherd than sit down at a mayoral banquet. I have no love for handmade artificial scenery, and that is why I avoid parks and public gardens. They are too refined and ladylike in dress, if scenery can be so described. I love wild flowers in fields, meadows, hedgerows and pools, all planted, nourished and tended by mother nature, better than I love flowers planted by man in prim formal beds. But

best of all, give me the wild gipsy like moor, with heather, cloud-
berry, bracken, and rolling miles of brown moorgrass to my knees,
and no living thing to see but wild birds and grey hares, and I
want no happier day.

A RHYME OF THE MOORS

I have moors in my blood they are my kin,
And my love for them so deeply bred in,
That oft as a lad with my father I'd go
At night to the moors for the morning, "crow".
And in after years how lightsome my feet,
Through ling and bracken and over the peat,
And over the miles of purple and green,
What songs I sung of good days I had seen.

I have seen morn come in a new gold gown
And trail it along over moorgrass brown,
I have seen grouse weddings on a May noon,
And watched eve give gold to the harvest moon.
I have felt to my face heather winds blow,
And waded in June through cotton grass snow,
And deep among bracken in summer time
I lay on green feathers dreaming of rhyme.

Dreaming of streams in their frolic and glee,
Singing and leaping down cloughs to the sea,
And dreams of birds that seemed friendly to me.
I've climbed crag castles with battlements high
Where the storms of winter wither and die,
And seen sorrowing moors all tears and pain
When rough winds lashed them with moorgrime and rain
And often I heard on the night roads lone,
How weird is the sound when the low winds moan.
I have stood by fires in old taprooms warm,
And dried my wet clothes and taken no harm.
When I had drained my pot of hot spiced ale
I said "Good night" and away o'er hill and dale.

YORKSHIRE OR LANCASHIRE

It has long been a query among journalists and others as to whether I am a Yorkshire or a Lancashire man. As I am not a notable literary figure with a national reputation, I fail to see how it matters where I hail from. However, if it is a matter of birth, I am a Yorkshireman, born near Friarmere Moor, in Saddleworth, but if it is a matter of appreciation, I believe I have had most from Lancashire, though I do not forget the appreciation I have received from my native Parish.

The following is from a "Yorkshire Post" review of one of my books :—

"Many records of Yorkshire village life have been compiled and attempts made by novelists and local historians to portray character and reproduce the idiom of Yorkshiremen, but rarely if ever has so arresting a picture of the habits and manners of the unsophisticated Yorkshireman been given as that which is disclosed in Ammon Wrigley's book. His characters stand out clean cut against a rugged background of moorland".

What appears below is from H. P. Kendall's "Halifax Hunts and Huntsmen" :—

"That inimitable and homespun Ammon Wrigley, has given us for all time a most vivid and living picture of sport and Yorkshire character in a Moorland township. I can only regret that our district has not produced a man like him—a man in touch and in sympathy with human nature who can raise the folk tales and songs above the nauseating fog that envelops the industrial community of Halifax to-day".

In August, 1938, I was claimed as a Yorkshireman. I received letters from Miss Phyllis Bentley in which she invited me to attend a gathering of Yorkshire Authors from all over England at the Great Northern Hotel, Leeds, and if I could not get back home they would put me up for the night. In one of her letters she said : "I am to reply to the toast 'Yorkshire' and we are hoping that you will speak in support". If there had been nothing else, that alone was enough to keep me in Oldham, for my public speaking is like Joe o' Johnny's throstle that sang inwardly. Just before the gathering took place I received a free ticket for the dinner from Miss Lettice Cooper and learned that all the authors had to wear a "Black Tie" to distinguish them from the guests, but I hadn't a tie of any kind or colour.

A love for the quiet ways of life has kept me away from many public functions and I replied to the two novelists thanking them and regretting that I could not accept their kind invitations. Sir Ben Turner sent me Leeds newspapers containing long illustrated reports of the dinner and the after proceedings. On reading them I felt glad that I had remained in Oldham for in addition to Miss Bentley and Miss Cooper, Miss Storm Jameson, Miss Naomi Jacobs, Mr. J. B. Priestley, Mr. Herbert Read and many other famous authors were present. They were too big for me and I should have felt utterly miserable and tongue-tied in their company. One newspaper picture showed the waiters carrying in the Yorkshire pudding and at that moment on the 8th of October, 1938, I sat in the Greaves Arms Hotel, Oldham, with the "drug of the easy heart", in my glass. My books are about a West Riding parish and I know little about the Yorkshire on the other side of Stanedge Moors.

Now what about Lancashire ? I am a member of the Lancashire Authors' Association and my prose and verse may be found in Lancashire Anthologies. Lectures on my work have been given in Manchester, Oldham, Rochdale and other Lancashire towns but none in Yorkshire. Mr Charles Owen's lecture was broadcast from Manchester and in it he said :—

> "Ammon Wrigley is a writer of uncommon individuality ; the man is seen behind the written word, who has given us in dialect and in ordinary English prose and verse of rare quality. He is master of a style simple, direct and plain. Yet capable of expressing a deep and poetic understanding of life and nature which is rare indeed to find".

The late Mr. William Beck of the Oldham Chronicle wrote much that is appreciative of my work.

"Ammon Wrigley has laughter and song in his heart. Now and again men are born that way. He is a man of the open air, the moors and valleys, and hills. He is not always of lightsome mind, he can pick out the salient points of life and character with an unerring sense of their true value. . . . The tender personal note is not lacking in his verses and sketches some of which in their local appeal are fine examples of choice, simple expression and deep feeling. The charm of his songs and poems woven out of long tramps in wind and sun and rain, homely talk and homely cheer by the ingle nook do not depend for their beauty on County boundaries. Some of them must have been wrought with the wind of the heath blowing round him. No idle singer of an empty day, he is one with men and Nature. With men in the simple natural emotions that do not change amidst the flux of time and circumstances, and one with nature by long communion and unspoiled love".

There is J. H. Swann's lecture before the Manchester Literary Club which is printed in the Club's Proceedings, and lectures by Mr. R. Kenney, Canon W. T. Taylor, and others.

The Fellowship was founded by Lancashire men and a few Saddleworth friends, and nearly all the members men and women are Lancashire people. There are a few members in the Colne Valley. Not long ago an Urban District Council near Manchester, built five rows of houses and named them after dialect writers. One is named Wrigley Crescent. I have not seen it but I am Lancashire there in stone or brick, and I have no quarrel with people who call me a mongrel, half Yorkshire and half Lancashire. I have often been described in the press as the Pennine poet and I have always disclaimed it. What I am appears in the Introduction.

CASTLESHAW VALLEY

A poem descriptive of the Castleshaw Valley, written about 1910.

The dear old days like jewels bright
   They sparkle around me still,
And shining through my inmost core,
   My eyes begin to fill.
With memory now I wander down
   The valley of the past,
And as each picture fades,—it leaves
   One fairer than the last.

So, to begin with I shall skip
   Just where the humour takes me,
And roam about and wander till
   The rhyming mood forsakes me.
By farm and cot and watermill
   By moorland stream and clough
By meadows lying fair and green,
   And pastures brown and rough.

Thro' Cudworth runs the sheep wall still,
   And o'er the Foxstone height
Above the bullet riddled bank
   The ancient target's site.
And now the spade has just revealed
   A truth half guessed before
A group of ancient furnaces
   With partly smelted ore.

Two moorland streams came splashing down
   The cloughs by Oaken Hill,
And wedded were, below the slope
   That looked on Broadhead Mill.
It was a plain three storeyed block
   A dam bank high and steep,
The very site now lies beneath
   The waters dark and deep.

ON STANEDGE MOOR

A famous place in bygone days
  For rosy speckled trout
They took one once so history says
  Twelve pounds or thereabouts.
Three days it lay at Broadhead
  Upon a great white dish,
And all the countryside came down
  To see the kingly fish.

And leaving here the brook went on
  Well fed by many a rill
And winding thro' a willow nook
  Went gaily past the lower mill.
A black and lonely ruin then,
  Where boggarts met at night,
We used to pass its frowning walls
  And shudder with affright.

A packhorse bridge across the stream
  A narrow strip of stone,
And just above a sheltered bank
  With strawberry overgrown.
And up and down the Broadhead cloughs
  The wild rose and woodbine grew
And all among the hazel boughs
  Their scented blossoms threw.

And here at least so history says,
  And history ought to know
That Billy Firth once kept a school
  Some eighty years ago.
Here oft has many a laggard youth
  Who took his learning slow,
Had all his lessons hammered in
  By Billy Firth's clog toe.

At Oaken Hill the garden fence
   A row of battered trees
A tale of desolation tells
   To every passing breeze.
And up across the benty fields
   The ruins of the Lee,
'Tis strange in twenty years or so
   What changes there can be.

Lowgate below the four lane ends
   A lonely ruin stands,
A merry place it once o'erlooked
   Its breezy pasture lands.
A chamber full of busy looms,
   When work was never "dree",
And there they wove the finest cloth
   After a hunting spree.

And Wood so famed in olden time
   For rare old English cheer,
An open door was kept for all
   The neighbours on Friarmere.
A buttery full of "souly" meats
   A cellar full of ales,
There are none such homesteads now
   In all the Saddleworth dales.

And here began a Sunday school
   The first the valley knew,
Before the school at Castleshaw
   Beside the moorland grew.
A little room with crooked walls,
   And not o'erstocked with light
Where little neighbour lads and maids
   Were taught to read and write.

And ever when I wander down
   Its long green avenue,
The scene around is hallowed with
   The happy days I knew.
Straightway down the meadows stand
   The waters deep and still
And half the grassy road is there
   That led down to the mill.

Woodtop was then a homely row
   The haunt of gradely men
Where Bonker brewed and Mally wove
   There stands a long sheep pen.
The ragged thorn so weather worn,
   The well across the lane,
Are all that speak of far off days
   That ne'er will come again.

The hollies down the driving gate
   With winter berries red,
Like all the kindly neighbour folk
   Are withered, bare and dead.
And lower down a field away
   Three little grassy dells
Where fairies danced on harvest nights
   And rang their tiny bells.

And Moorcroft woods lay just below,
   A warm and pleasant nook,
With meadows sloping gently down,
   And fields across the brook.
And round about its gables ran
   And sparkled many a rill,
That gathering by the hedgerow side
   Went down by Moorcroft mill.

The ivied gable green and thick,
  The hawthorn edges rich,
The little pools with cresses strewn,
  The foxglove down the ditch.
A place old custom ne'er forsook,
  But dwelt there all its days,
The sturdy yoeman stamped his foot
  On all new fangled ways.

Up and down the mill folks went,
  Ever passing to and fro,
With woven ends and "pokes" of weft
  "Brawson" weavers walking slow.
Two slubbers meeting at the door
  And "stroddlin" there together,
Taking snuff and talking loud
  Of cattle, work and weather.

Now all are gone and swept away,
  No stick or stone are left,
Nothing now to show where stood,
  That busy place of warp and weft.
And what a cheery spot it was,
  The merriest in the dale,
When one looks back, it only seems
  A simple fairy tale.

TOWN AND COUNTRY

"I COULDN'T live on your hills", she said,
  "They're bare and cold to me,
Give me the town, the pleasant shops,
  And pretty gowns to see".

"If I should climb your dirty moors
  I know they'd hurt my feet,
I'd rather go with folks at eve
  Shop gazing through the street".

100

"The picture houses thronged at night,
  The film stars lovely things,
With powdered cheeks and painted lips
  Are angels without wings".

"The dance halls full of pretty girls,
  The music, life and swing;
And you go out of doors to hear
  A silly skylark sing".

"You country folks are half asleep
  No matter what you think;
You've no fine rooms where folks like me
  Smoke cigarettes and drink".

"And as for colour, see the shops
  Ablaze with ribbons bright,
And all you see are dreary fields
  And stone walls black as night".

"Your coloured ribbons, miss", I said,
  "Are woven in a loom;
'Tis God who weaves on Alderman,
  When heather is in bloom".

"There is a kind of beauty dear,
  God never takes to town;
When bracken's gold in Wessenden,
  And Lingreave's russet brown".

"He has a shop at Easter Gate,
  And one at South Clough Head;
And one not far from Isle of Skye
  When cloudberries are red".

101

"God does not offer gowns for sale
   He gives to all who care ;
You cannot put them on your back,
   They're for your soul to wear".

"You'll see Him in the April fields
   When they are flower strewn ;
And in the hawthorns on a hedge
   On blossom days in June".

"You to your streets and fashion shops,
   Your painted film stars too ;
But I who love the lonely hills,
   Will never change with you".

THE DALESMAN.

I MET a dalesman in the town,
   Though wintry cold to me,
He'd summer weather on his face,
   As brown as berries be :

His neck was red with farmer's fare,
   Roast beef and home baked bread,
"Ther's nowt licks livin' weel, owd lad,
   An' lyin' warm", he said.

"An old song of the dales", I said,
   "Is in that twang of thine ;
That ever goes deep down in me
   And warms my heart like wine ;

A song that comes from upland farms,
   From cart ruts up a lane ;
From old hay barns and shippon folds,
   And cows out in the rain.

The country sounds are in thy voice,
   The gentle and the rough ;
The sound of waters splashing o'er
   The boulders down a clough.

The wuther of the wild March wind,
   The throstle's April tune ;
The sound of mowers whetting scythes,
   On haytime morns in June.

The low of cows at milking time,
   The hounds out on a hill ;
And every word that leaves thy tongue
   Hath magic for me still".

AT THE RISING OF THE SUN

CLIMBING the fields to the moor height,
I saw the stars flee with the night,
   At the rising of the sun :
A new born day is joy to see,
Like all young things it is to me
The fairest in its infancy,
   At the rising of the sun.

A frolic wind begins to sing,
As it comes leaping o'er the ling ;
   At the rising of the sun :
And in the moor grass brown and deep,
The little things that fly or creep,
Turn in their beds and wake from sleep,
   At the rising of the sun.

The birds awake the curlews rise,
And soaring cleave the golden skies ;
   At the rising of the sun :
And on the knolls as I draw near
The moorcocks calling loud and clear
G-bak ! g-bak ! the morn is here,
   At the rising of the sun.

Oh happy morns when day begins,
Far from the town and all its sins,
    At the rising of the sun :
From squalid slum and drab main street,
From noise of wheels and tramp of feet,
And you so clean and fresh and sweet,
    At the rising of the sun.

A SPRINGTIME LETTER

OH, here is Mollie's letter,
    She writes a dainty hand ;
It looks as though a fairy
    Had waved its little wand.

She says "I've seen a swallow
    And heard a linnet sing ;
There's blossom on the blackthorn,
    And everywhere is spring".

"It is a lovely morning,
    The night has left no dregs,
And every bit of heaven
    Is blue as throstle eggs".

"I'm writing by a window,
    And looking out I see
A little mist of greenery
    Upon a cherry tree".

"A golden rain of kingcups,
    Has fallen by the stream ;
And in the primrose hollows
    There's April spilling cream".

"There'll soon be blossom hedges,
    About the end of May,
With trees as white as bridesmaids
    Upon a wedding day".

"I see the sunny hayfield,
  Where we'd a jolly tea ;
I think of Jean and wonder
  If she remembers me".

"She's married now and children,
  And something else to do
Than leaping over haycocks
  And racing me and you".

"Our maids are busy cleaning,
  The milkman says, "yor thrung",
And mother's got rheumatic,
  But it isn't in her tongue".

"You know she calls me madcap,
  But of course I don't care,
Why should I ? free and happy
  Out in the open air".

"Remember me to Sallie,
  Her with the bluest eyes ;
You're blest to have a sister
  So bonnie and so wise".

"So goodbye, dearest Helen,
  Oh, mother's calling me ;
She says, 'go clean the silver',
  I'm off along the lea".

THE ROAMER'S RETURN

HOME to dear old Saddleworth, home once more,
How my heart is stirred to its inmost core ;
For I've been roaming and it's joy to go
Up the hillside lane by the fields I know.

105

Home to the hamlet where my own folks bide,
To the old armchair by the hearthstone side ;
To the neighbour folks and my boyhood's friends,
Who oft played with me at the old lane ends.

Home to the throstle on the high ash tree,
When its throat is full of the springtime glee ;
To the upland fields where the skylarks sing,
And the rough brown moor with its grouse and ling.

Home to the meadows in the mowing time,
To the high barn now that I used to climb ;
To the windrows turned on a housing day,
And the laneside trees hung with wisps of hay.

I'll go to the village not far below,
To the quaint old street and folks I know ;
I know what they'll say as they've always done :
"Put it theer, owd lad, if it weighs a ton".

The little sweet shop where I used to stare
At the parkin pigs and toffy sticks there ;
How I pressed my nose 'gainst the window pane,
And longed for a penny but longed in vain.

Home to old Saddleworth what more do I need,
Than the hills I love and the men they breed ?
And I'll roam no more for I ne'er have found
More kindlier hearts or a dearer ground.